JOHN KEEGAN

WAR AND OUR WORLD

John Keegan was for many years senior lecturer
in military history at the Royal Military
Academy, Sandhurst, and has been a fellow at
Princeton University and a professor of history at
Vassar College. He is the author of fourteen
previous books, including the acclaimed *The Face
of Battle* and *The Second World War* and, most
recently, *The First World War,* a national best-
seller. In May 2000 he was knighted for services
to military history. He lives in Wiltshire,
England.

WAR
AND OUR
WORLD

JOHN KEEGAN

VINTAGE BOOKS
A Division of Random House, Inc.
New York

FIRST VINTAGE BOOKS EDITION, JUNE 2001

Copyright © 1998 by John Keegan

All rights reserved under International and Pan-American Copyright
Conventions. Published in the United States by Vintage Books, a division of
Random House, Inc., New York. Originally published in hardcover in Great
Britain by Hutchinson, London, in 1998.

Vintage and colophon are registered trademarks of Random House, Inc.

Library of Congress Cataloging-in-Publication Data
Keegan, John, 1934–
War and our world / John Keegan.
p. cm. — (The Reith Lectures ; 1998)
Originally published: London : Hutchinson, 1998.
Includes bibliographical references.
ISBN 0-375-70520-1 (pbk.)
1. War and society. 2. War. I. Title. II. Series.
HM554.K44 2001
303.6'6—dc21   00-067410
CIP

www.vintagebooks.com

Printed in the United States of America
10 9 8 7 6 5 4 3 2 1

ACKNOWLEDGEMENTS

I am grateful to all those at the BBC who helped in the preparation and delivery of these lectures, particularly Anne Winder, Head of Topical Features, Keith Jones, my endlessly painstaking producer, Anne Smith, his assistant, Carole Haynes, who arranged for the invitation of the audiences and James Boyle, who extended to me the invitation to deliver the 1998 Reith Lectures in the first place. I would also like to thank the outside broadcasting teams who recorded the lectures at the Royal Institution, the Royal Military Academy Sandhurst, King's College London and the University of Glasgow, and the Commandant, Principal and Vice-Chancellor of the last three who welcomed the BBC to their institutions.

Mrs Lindsey Wood typed and edited the manuscripts and, as always, I give her my deepest thanks. I would also like to thank my editor at Hutchinson, Anthony Whittome, who arranged for the publication of the lectures in this form and against severe pressure of time. My wife and children know my gratitude to them.

For permission to quote the poem 'To My Son' by
Rudyard Kipling, the author and publishers thank
A. P. Watt acting for the National Trust.

CONTENTS

INTRODUCTION

WHY WAR? THE QUESTION IS double-edged. I do not know why men fight wars, though I make an attempt to sketch an answer in the pages that follow. Why the 1998 Reith Lectures are about war is more easily explained. When, to my great surprise, James Boyle, the Controller of BBC Radio 4, asked me, in the spring of 1997, to deliver the lectures, he began by leaving the subject to my choice. I reflected at length and proposed some ideas at our second meeting. None, at least directly, was about war. After hearing me out, he said gently that he thought I would find I would speak best about what I knew best. So war was selected as the subject.

Yet I do not, of course, know about war in any direct way at all. Disabled by a childhood illness, I have not served in any of the armed forces and my exposure to the scenes of war have been brief and distant. As a war correspondent I visited the Lebanon in 1983 and the Gulf – before the outbreak of the fighting – in 1990, and I have also reported from Northern Ireland, the North-West Frontier and South Africa during times of troubles. Except in the Lebanon, I was never in the slightest danger. My knowledge of war is therefore second-hand and academic, largely acquired in the library of the Royal Military Academy Sandhurst during the years I spent there between 1960 and 1985, teaching military history to the future officers of the British Army.

Sandhurst was, nevertheless, a true education in war. The spirit and routine of the Academy taught me military discipline, for we worked long hours to a strict timetable which did not indulge the individual. The day was not nine-to-five nor were the weekends necessarily one's own. During one period of reorganisation, even annual leave was abolished. I thus learnt that, in the army, time to oneself is a privilege, not a right, and that duty to the institution takes precedence over other obligations.

I would in any case have learnt that from the company of the soldiers who were my colleagues. In the 1960s Sandhurst was staffed by officers who had fought either in the Second World War or in the campaigns that followed it. Most had decorations for bravery in the face of the enemy. They were a light-hearted collection of human beings, with a refreshingly self-confident attitude to authority. To the principle of authority and to the demands it made on their lives, they shared, however, an automatic respect. Having braved death and seen men die, they understood in their bones that it was only the habit of obedience and the automatic performance of orders that made an army work and spared life that would be lost by prevarication or dispute. Their ethic was even stronger than that. Professional officers, I learned to recognise, regarded the discharge of duty as a matter of personal honour. To fail in duty was to dishonour themselves as individuals and, by extension, the body of comrades to which they belonged. Dishonour was so disgraceful that it was preferable to risk death itself rather than be marked by that taint.

To the question 'Why war?', therefore, Sandhurst supplied the answer that the professional soldiers of constitutional states fight wars because it is their duty to do so. That was not an answer to the larger question, 'Why do wars happen at all?' There are few constitutional states in the world, fewer that maintain professional armies and, among those, still fewer that observe the high standards of duty and morality characteristic of the British in our time. Historically, war has been a dirty business, in which professional armies have been minority participants. If we date the origin of war to the fourth millennium BC, most of the wars fought in the ensuing five thousand years have made little place for the man of honour, the high-minded warrior. The aristocrat in arms, the knight of chivalry, the gentleman officer figure prominently in the chronicles of war, whether they come down to us from the early Chinese empire, the high Middle Ages or the dynastic conflicts of monarchical Europe. All have been outnumbered by the brutish rank-and-file, the conscript dolt, the mercenary, the free-booting predator of the cavalry horde or the raiding longship.

War, historically, is a predatory affair. The most likely explanation of its origin is in the attacks made by our hunter ancestors on our other ancestors who, after the retreat of the glaciers at the end of the last ice age, had begun to domesticate animals and cultivate the land. These early pastoralists and farmers made easy meat. It was only slowly that they learnt to protect themselves against the raiders who emerged without warning from the wilderness beyond the borders of the cultivated lands to pillage and slay. The first form of protection they adopted was that of fortification. When the limited value of fixed defences was recognised, they began to take the offensive to the enemy. Armies originated as counter-attack forces, funded out of the agricultural surplus, which paid some of the early agricultural communities' members to undertake specialist, perhaps full-time duty as soldiers. By the third millennium BC, such military specialists were campaigning at long distance from cultivated land to check raiders at the borders and even carry war into their homelands.

It was to be a long step, however, between the inception of purposive warfare and the domination of human communities by specialist armed forces. Civilisation, which depends for its survival on the maintenance of law and order, within and without, is a fragile creation. Between the invention of the first regular armies in the first millennium BC and their universal adoption by the world's advanced states only three hundred years ago, much disorder intervened. The Chinese empire, oldest and most durable of polities, underwent frequent periods of turmoil whenever its armies lost control of the border with Central Asia or of the population. Rome, which perfected the regular army in a form still influential today, succeeded in establishing stability and maintaining it for several hundred years. It did so, however, only by conducting an active defence of the frontiers as a permanent condition of the empire's survival and, when the army eventually failed as an instrument of state, disorder broke in, to persist over wide areas of Europe for a thousand years.

In the wider world, untouched by the Roman or Chinese empires, warfare was endemic, motivated often by predation but also, as society complexified, by quarrels over personal, family or group prestige, territorial control, access to markets or commodities or by the need to achieve security. All those motives are discernible in the military history of the Greek world, with its passion for discord. Quarrel over rights, legal or dynastic, was a particular cause of warfare in post-Roman Europe. To these impulses to belligerence the rise of Islam, in the seventh century AD, added that of demand for religious conformity, not previously known as a military imperative. It would eventually become a major cause of conflict, as would, later still, political ideologies that claimed a similar orthodoxy.

The rise of the European maritime empires in the eighteenth and nineteenth centuries had the indirect effect, meanwhile, of bringing local and traditional warfare over much of Asia and Africa to an end. Whatever its injustices, imperialism brought domestic peace to Europe's colonies and possessions. Paradoxically, it was within Europe, after a comparatively untroubled nineteenth century, that war returned to rend civilised life with an intensity never before known. The First World War shook the continent's political structure to its foundations, destroying historic dynastic states and creating circumstances in which aggressive ideologies came to rule where comparatively benevolent monarchies had done before. The Second World War, essentially a conflict of those ideologies, broke continental borders to engulf eventually almost the whole world and to carry to its far corners the most destructive military technology human ingenuity could invent, of which the atomic bomb was the ultimate development. By 1945 the many transformations through which war had passed had culminated in a form of war mankind could no longer risk waging. Hiroshima and Nagasaki were not simply military events but warnings that warfare was now a medium of human relations that would destroy all who tried to turn it to their use.

'Why war?' was therefore a question no longer

worth asking, except in a historical context, because war waged with the worst of available weapons was henceforth nonsensical. The question 'How war?' nevertheless remained. Paradoxically, as responsible statesmen everywhere recognised, nuclear war could be averted only if a way could be found to use military force as a restraint against seekers after power who threatened the general peace. Thankfully thus far in the nuclear age, such ways have been found. A conclusive solution has not, nor, one must realise, will it ever be. 'The condition of liberty is eternal vigilance': all reasonable people desire liberty from the threat of war. It can be assured only by the devotion to duty of democracy's professional warriors. They deserve our respect, trust and support.

WAR AND OUR WORLD

CHAPTER ONE
WAR AND OUR WORLD

WAR HAS BEEN THE SCOURGE of this century. The ride of the other three horsemen of the Apocalypse, and particularly famine and pestilence, has been halted and even turned back during the last ninety years. Nowhere in the world is starvation unavoidable, while the diseases that killed our forebears in millions – plague, cholera and typhus foremost among them – are almost forgotten afflictions. It is war that has replaced them as an enemy of human life, well-being, happiness and optimism. The effect of war on the lives of human individuals and the communities in which they live is the theme of these lectures.

Much of what I have to say dwells on war's scourge-like nature and on the way in which, from small beginnings, war came in our own century to threaten the survival of civilisation itself. I hope, however, to lead my audience to conclude, as I do, that the worst of war is now behind us and that mankind, with vigilance and resolution, will henceforth be able to conduct the affairs of the world in a way that allows war a diminishing part.

The First World War killed at least ten million people in battle, most of them young or very young men, and millions more died from war-related causes. The Second World War killed fifty million, of whom fewer than half were servicemen in uniform. Yugoslavia, for example, lost ten per cent of its population, of which but a fraction belonged to the Royal Yugoslav Army; the rest died as a result of deprivation, reprisal or internecine massacre.

The toll of war persisted beyond the great peace of 1945. Civil war and wars of national liberation, in China, Vietnam, Algeria, the Middle East, Angola and Mozambique, and the inter-ethnic wars that have followed the dissolution of empires, are often calculated to have killed another fifty million. How conscious we all are of the killings that have affronted civilised sentiment in this decade, the killings in Rwanda and Bosnia that have added another million victims to the century's casualty list.

Demographers explain that human fertility soon replaces the war dead. No war anywhere, except the Paraguayan war of 1864–70, has ever equalled or even approached the lethality of the Black Death, which killed one European in four in the fourteenth century. Birth rates rapidly recover, as they did even in Paraguay, which lost nine-tenths of its males, and populations continue to increase.

If the costs of war were measured solely in statistics, they could indeed be shrugged off. The costs, however, are not measured only on graphs. The unquantifiable cost is in emotional suffering, by which the pain of one death is often multiplied many times, through the network of family relationships, and in long-term, indeed lifelong, deprivation.

Even demographers admit that war losses cause a generational imbalance between the sexes. In Germany in 1945, the imbalance between males and females of marriageable age stood at 100:180, which denied hundreds of thousands of German women any prospect of marriage or re-marriage. The imbalance in the Soviet Union, which had lost ten, rather than four, million soldiers, was higher still.

The emotional cost of war has, moreover, been heightened in this century in a peculiarly excruciating way. The wounds of war are always self-inflicted, unlike those caused by disease, against which mankind struggled in vain for millennia. Traditionally imprecise and long-delayed, news of the death in war of someone dear was accompanied by the eternal and consequent 'why?' asked by those who heard of it, to which have been added in our time the long-drawn-out apprehensions of 'will it be us?' and, if so, 'when?'

Ours has been, we constantly congratulate ourselves, the news century. The news-gatherer has become a modern celebrity and the means by which he transmits what he learns, the telegraph, radio, television, and now fax and e-mail, are among our chief modern marvels. News is today a welcome and almost

necessary commodity, even if it is bad, as it decreas-
ingly often is, for someone else.

What the permeation of our consciousness by constant reportage has led us to forget is that, for several
long periods during the lifetime of people still alive,
news was what they did not want to hear. The telegraph boy on his bicycle, pedalling the suburban street
and symbol to the Victorians of a new and benevolent
technological advance, became for parents and wives
during both world wars literally an omen of terror – for
it was by telegram that the awful flimsy form beginning
'We regret to inform you that' was brought to front
doors, a trigger for the articulation of the constant
unspoken prayer, 'Let him pass by, let him stop at
another house, let it not be us.'

In Britain during the First World War that prayer
was not answered several million times; on seven hundred thousand occasions the telegraph boy brought the
ultimate bad news of the death of a son, husband or
brother. 'We are dreading the Telegram that so many
have received lately,' wrote Robert Saunders, a fort-
night after the opening of the battle of the Somme, in
which his son was serving, and already twenty thousand young British soldiers had been killed.*

'The terror by day', as the wartime telegram has
been called, could inflict direct, immediate and inextin-
guishable pain simply by what it told. Patrick Dalziel-

*Quoted in Trevor Wilson, *The Myriad Faces of War* (Blackwell/Polity,
1986, p. 389).

Job, a Second World War naval officer, describes how, as a young and only child, he heard the news of his father's death in the First World War.

He was playing with a mechanical toy in the space between the bed and the wall in a rented seaside room which his mother had taken while his father was away at the front. She was brushing her hair, silhouetted against the window. While she brushed it, she told him that Daddy would not be coming back from the war. She continued to brush her hair. After an interval, he resumed play with his mechanical toy. His mother, who was still young during the Second World War, did not remarry.

Sometimes the telegram tortured because the news it brought was imprecise. 'Down on your knees, Julia, and thank God you haven't a son,' said Rudyard Kipling to a friend while he waited to hear news of his only son, John, reported missing after the battle of Loos in September 1915.*

For months he and Carrie, his wife, kept up hope that John might be a prisoner. Carrie hoped longer than Rudyard. Eventually he wrote a short poem of acceptance that John was dead:

> My son was killed while laughing at some jest.
> I would I knew
> What it was and it might serve me in a time
> When jests are few.†

*Angus Wilson, *The Strange Ride of Rudyard Kipling* (Pimlico, 1994, p. 304).
†Quoted, ibid. p. 305.

Kipling deluded himself, or perhaps was deluded by one of the many Irish Guardsmen from whom he sought word of his son's fate. His friend, Rider Haggard, who had met the last of John's comrades to see him alive, knew that he was then crying in pain from a wound in the mouth.

Where and when John later died, no one can tell. He was one of the five hundred thousand British soldiers of the Great War whose bodies were lost in the wasteland of shattered trenches and crater fields which battle left behind. Ironically, as we now know, his remains were eventually discovered, and re-interred under a headstone bearing the words Rudyard Kipling had himself composed to commemorate the missing, 'Known Unto God'.

Sometimes, finally, the telegram tortured, with fatal effect, even if it did not come at all. Let me give an example. It is one of the tragedies of the twentieth century that most mature adults have a war story, good sometimes, bad more often. Here is a bad one of my own. I did not know my paternal grandmother, who died many years before I was born, in the winter of 1917.

At the time my father was an eighteen-year-old gunner, serving in a battery near Arras, on the Western Front. On hearing that his mother was gravely ill, he was sent home on compassionate leave but arrived too late. A neighbour met him as he walked from the station to the family house and unwittingly commiserated with him on his bereavement. He told me the story among his carefully censored war memories. But later, when he was himself near death, he revealed a little more. That summer, as his mother had taken him to the station to see him off to France in his new khaki, she had broken down. 'I shall never see you again,' she said.

I wondered – continue to wonder – at the depth of anguish that could have torn such words from a loving parent at such a moment. My father's sister, one of the army of spinsters left by the Great War, added some explanation towards the end of her own life. She had seen her three brothers go to the war, Richard in 1915, Edward in 1916. 'When Frank went in 1917,' she said, 'the worry began to consume mother. She wasn't really very ill that winter. She just gave up the ghost.'

So a mother had frightened herself to death, as if to fulfil the awful prophecy dragged out of her on the railway platform from which she sent her youngest off to the carnage. Ironically again, all three brothers came safely back, physically almost untouched, from their years in the trenches.

I offer this small family reminiscence not for its personal but for its universal significance. That is a theme taken up by George MacDonald Fraser in his wonderful memoir of service in the Border Regiment in Burma in 1944–5. Throughout he was acutely conscious of the risks he ran; two of his nine immediate comrades were indeed killed in what he calls 'the lottery of active service'.

In reflection, however, it is with those in England that he most strongly identifies. 'Whatever anxieties the soldier may experience in the field can be nothing to the torment of those at home . . . Those months must have been the longest of [my parents'] lives.'*

The point he is seeking to make, I think, is that soldiers know when and why they have reason to be in fear, which typically is not very often – war service has been called 'long periods of boredom punctuated by moments of acute terror'. Yet those who worry for them do so every waking hour. In this century, moreover, endemic anxiety has been an emotion of majorities throughout Europe, North America, much of Asia and Australasia and parts of Africa for very long periods.

Why was that? George MacDonald Fraser again illuminates. On hearing news of the outbreak of the Second World War, his grandmother remarked, 'Well, the men will be going away again'.† Her matter-of-fact acceptance of a reality she correctly anticipated reminds us that advanced states had achieved in her lifetime what none had previously succeeded in doing: making every man a soldier.

Traditionally, armies were hard to assemble. Soldiers might be hired, but at such cost that price kept mercenary armies small. They could be employed on

---

*George MacDonald Fraser, *Quartered Safe Out Here* (Harvill, 1992, p. 73).
†Ibid.

long-term contract, as regulars, but the expense of regular armies kept them small also. By means still difficult to dissect, during the nineteenth century nation states managed to persuade their populations that all fit males should undergo military training in early manhood; furthermore, that afterwards they should hold themselves in readiness to return to service when called.

Conscript service produced large, relatively cheap peacetime armies, while the reserve obligation promised to produce very large wartime ones. We can understand some of the mechanisms that assisted that process. The institution of the census supplied the names and addresses of those of military age. The introduction of compulsory education disciplined the potential recruits and fitted them for training. Meanwhile the rise of factory work, itself a disciplinary influence, yielded both the goods necessary to arm and equip the conscript millions and the wealth that could be taxed to pay for them. Yet what these developments do not explain is why populations, separate from states, consented to raise the enormous armies that, twice in this century worldwide, and regionally more often than that, have inflicted such an emotional burden on those who assented to, or at least acquiesced, in their creation.

All we can say is that they did. Historians recognise that there was a 'militarisation' of Europe in the last century, one effect of which was to represent the performance of military service as an honourable duty all ought to undertake and the maintenance of big armies – and navies – as a good thing. The military mood persisted into the first half of this century, and that mood combined with the very large available numbers of fighting men to generate battles on a scale and of a duration never before known.

We now call them battles of attrition – Passchendaele and Verdun are examples from the First World War, Stalingrad and Normandy from the Second. Attrition is the process in which the infliction of casualties on constantly replaced numbers is protracted until the resolution of one side or the other breaks. Yet the paradox was that generals, and states, had argued for large armies because numbers were supposed to bring quick and cheap victories.

When eventually they produced only long casualty lists, that outcome was rationalised as a necessary means to victory. When populations began to question whether victory was worth the price – as the British and French did after 1918 – we can begin to identify a reversal of the military mood that captured Europe in the nineteenth century.

Moods, however, are difficult to change, and they alter erratically over time and from place to place. Only after 1945 did the Germans and Japanese decide that the quest for victory had cost an unbearable price. American military triumphalism was thrown into reverse only by the crisis of the Vietnam war and not until this decade did a new generation of North

Vietnamese begin to question whether a conflict that killed two hundred thousand of their young men each year between 1966 and 1972 was really worth fighting.

I have spoken so far only of the human cost of war, and largely of the emotional effect of that cost on our world. I am prepared to justify that bias, for material damage is more easily and quickly made good than emotional loss, which never can be. Nevertheless, we must remember that the material damage caused by the Second World War in particular was as unparalleled in scale as the loss of life in both world wars and that the effort to repair it distorted normal economic activity for decades.

A striking example of how great was the material loss caused by the Second World War is presented by the case of the United States. In 1939 the American economy was the largest in the world, as it had been since the late nineteenth century. By 1945 the American national product was equal in value to that of the rest of the world put together.

Spared the effects of strategic bombing, blockade and fighting over its territory between 1941 and 1945, the United States had been able to raise both domestic consumption and industrial output, to maximise agricultural yields, to modernise its infrastructure, to increase exploitation of its readily available natural resources without exhausting them, and still, by the war's end, to have accumulated a fiscal surplus which alone offered hope of providing the investment necessary to repair the catastrophic damage inflicted by war on other economies, those of friend and foe alike, exposed to every one of the calamities it had avoided. •

The calamities suffered by the defeated were calamities indeed. The centre of all Germany's largest cities had been bombed flat or burnt out, and as many as a million German civilians, the majority women and children, had been killed under air attack; to return for a moment to the emotional dimension of the war, many of the four million German soldiers killed in action must have fought their last battles afflicted by the worry of whether their loved ones lived or not.

This is not to solicit special sympathy for the nation that had initiated the war. It is merely to recognise that Germany was the most heavily bombed country among the combatants. Materially the Japanese suffered even worse. During 1945, sixty per cent of the ground area of Japan's sixty largest cities was burnt out, incidentally killing more civilians than in the atomic bombings of Hiroshima and Nagasaki in August.

During 1945, normal economic life in Germany and Japan was brought to a halt and their populations were fed in defeat by the charity of their enemies. In the Soviet Union, a victor nation, economic activity had declined by two-thirds, while in Britain victory brought even slimmer rations than had passed the U-boat blockade.

In every major combatant country, except the

United States, years of unproductive military expenditure and of under-investment in the civilian economy, often no investment at all, condemned the peoples who welcomed the peace to a new round of economic self-denial in the cause of repairing the war's self-inflicted wounds.

Some wounds could not be repaired. The cultural damage caused by the war included the destruction of much of the built heritage of England, Germany and Austria, often in reprisal bombing raids, and the deliberate devastation of such sites as the Russian and German imperial palaces, the old city of Warsaw, and the abbey of Monte Cassino, mother house of European monasticism; there was, as well, much collateral damage to the architectural heritage of Italy, France and the Low Countries.

Among the art treasures destroyed, or lost for years without trace as a result of private or official looting, were the contents of the great Berlin museums, stored in the city's flak towers; a fire in the Friedrichshain flak tower on May 6, 1945, destroyed 434 Old Master paintings, including works by Botticelli, Caravaggio, Titian, Veronese and Rubens and such German masters as Cranach and Menzel.

War has always been destructive of treasure; the journey of the famous horses of St Mark, which have wandered since the Fourth Crusade between Constantinople, Venice, Paris and Venice again, is a cautionary survival story. War has also always been destructive of life.

The point towards which I have been striving, however, and on which I want to conclude is this: war, until very recent times, was not among life's great enemies. Famine, yes; fear of famine was among the causes of the French Revolution, the event from which we date the beginning of the modern world. Disease, too; plague, cholera and typhus regularly killed millions more than wars ever did until those of the French Revolution and perhaps afterwards. War had previously had occasional epidemic effects, as during the Thirty Years War of the seventeenth century.

Yet a visitation from that particular apocalyptic horseman always stood lower in mankind's fears than those of the arbitrary and impersonal arrival of successful germs or of the failure of crops. The fear of war as a widespread killer first began to afflict families only in the nineteenth century – first of all, I think, in the United States during the American Civil War, as lines from Walt Whitman's poem 'Come Up from the Fields Father' so piercingly convey –

> See, dearest mother, the letter says Pete will soon
> be better
> Alas poor boy, he will never be better

Only in the twentieth century did the fear of war finally overtake in force the primordial anxieties associated with deprivation and sickness.

Ironically, or paradoxically – I recognise that I have employed both words before – the appalling cost of warfare achieved in the twentieth century is the outcome of an exactly contrary aspiration. Automatic weapon fire, massed artillery bombardment, aerial bombing, unpiloted missiles and ultimately nuclear and thermonuclear weapons – almost every single one of the century's so-called advances in military technology or practice – was conceived and developed as a means of sparing loss of life, at least to one's own side.

That they too often resulted not in quick and cheap victory but in bloody attrition cannot deny that incontestable fact. How did it come about that a man-made affliction, war, has only quite recently succeeded in replacing the calamities of the natural world as our chief life-threatening phenomenon? How, indeed, did war begin in the first place? Those questions will be the subject of my next two lectures.

CHAPTER TWO
THE ORIGINS OF WAR

WAR, AS I ARGUED IN my first lecture, has overtaken disease and famine in the hierarchy of threats this world offers to human life, liberty and happiness only in very recent times. We must be realistic. Life itself is a dangerous and ultimately fatal condition. We are all going to die. No one in Britain today, however, fears death by starvation and it is safe to predict that a relatively small proportion of people in the world will die for lack of food in what remains of this century. Such assumptions mark a revolutionary shift in expectations, for even in eighteenth-century France, then the richest country in Europe, rich and poor alike waited on tenterhooks for the next harvest, the poor because they might not survive a hunger winter, the rich because the hungry might rise in revolution.

Our assumptions about the menace of disease have altered also. As late as the early decades of this century, even the very rich were stalked by fear of infections that the most expensive medicine could not hold at bay, while the passage from life to death was associated not only with squalor and indignity but often with uncontrollable pain.

Such fears have largely left us, but the fear of war will not go away. Indeed, because war has got worse, so has our fear of what it threatens. That fear may for the moment, to borrow a term from medicine, be in remission. The end of the Cold War, the relaxation of nuclear confrontation, have taken military crisis from the front page. Nevertheless, we are nagged by the anxiety that the absence of bad news will not last – we cannot speak of good news in a decade during which television has brought us the scenes of massacre in Rwanda and Bosnia.

That is not unreasonable. Rational judgement underpins our altered attitudes to sickness and want. Man has equally rational reasons for mistrusting the power of reason to control human behaviour. While we recognise that it is irrational to risk nuclear punishment in a world dominated by nuclear weapons, we recognise equally that we are a risk-taking species. In a sense, we know ourselves too well to feel confidence in the hope that man will behave any better in the future than he did in the past. We suspect that there is something ineradicable in ourselves, or in the way we organise our lives together, or perhaps in both, that makes general war, sometime, somewhere, inevitable. What can we say about the origins of war?

Little that will not cause conflict between scholars. Students of the origins of war broadly divide into those who look for evidence of it embedded in human nature and those who seek it among the external or contingent influences which act upon human nature. The naturalists, as the first group is known, divide further, and with marked hostility. A minority of them insist that man is naturally violent, as many animal species are. The majority, by contrast, regard violence as an aberrant, unnatural activity, to be found only in flawed individuals or as a response to particular sorts of provocation or stimulation, and therefore avoidable if such triggers can be identified and palliated or eliminated.

The strength of feeling on the subject among the naturalist majority is exemplified by what has become their loyalty test, the Seville Statement of May 1986, modelled on UNESCO's Statement on Race, and now adopted by the American Anthropological Association as its official position. The Statement contains five articles, each prefaced by the words, 'It is scientifically incorrect'.*

Thus if one subscribes to the Seville Statement, it is scientifically incorrect to believe that 'we have inherited a tendency to make war from our animal ancestors', or to believe that 'war or any other violent behaviour is genetically programmed into our human nature'. It also asserts that is is scientifically incorrect to believe that 'in the course of human evolution there has been a

*The Seville Statement, *Anthropology Today*, June 1989, Vol. 5, No. 3, p. 2

selection for aggressive behaviour more than for other kinds of behaviour', that 'humans have a "violent" brain' or, finally, to believe that 'war is caused by "instinct" or any other single motivation'.

There is much to be admired about the Seville Statement, since it seeks to liberate the human race from the deadening conviction that war is its natural lot. Unfortunately, there is little that is scientific about it. Science has thus far quite failed to substantiate any of its five articles, some of which are not scientific propositions at all.

Animals do not make war. They kill to eat, even if occasionally in a wasteful 'feeding frenzy'. War is too complex an activity for step-by-step genetic mutation to 'program' organisms for it; and geneticists lack the evidence to strike a balance between selection for this behaviour or that within the vast human behavioural range. The Seville Statement, in short, is one of hope, not objective truth. Objectively, all that science has been able to establish about human nature and war is the whereabouts in the human brain of what scientists call 'the seat of aggression' and how it may be stimulated or physically altered to produce aggressive behaviour.

The seat of aggression, known as the limbic system, is located low in the central brain and contains three groups of cells, the hypothalamus, the septum and the amygdala. Each group alters behaviour when it is damaged or electrically stimulated, but not in a uniform way. If, for example, part of the hypothalamus of a male rat is damaged, the rat becomes less aggressive. Electrical stimulation of it, on the other hand, makes the rat more aggressive, though only towards less dominant rats. This pattern is discernible in other species, and suggests that the direction of aggression is controlled by a higher part of the brain, the frontal lobes, where incoming sensations are processed.

Fear may be a product of such processing, but so also is prudence, and each sensation is communicated from the frontal lobes to the limbic system by hormonal or neural transmitters. When the appropriate hormones or stimulants are applied to the limbic system they produce more aggressive behaviour; however no experiment has yet followed the processing of incoming sensations in all its complexity through to the final transmitting outcome. We simply do not know, therefore, how the limbic system responds to the frontal lobes and so cannot say whether, by analogy from animals, man is more rational than instinctive or the other way about. The neural origins of aggression have not been clarified.

Genetics is more revealing. More rather than less aggressive individuals are identifiable in many species and breeding for aggression can transmit that characteristic. Fighting bulls, for example, are bred by selection. We also know that certain chromosome patterns in humans are associated with aggressive behaviour and that the group of one in a thousand males that inherits two rather than one Y chromosome yields a slightly higher and disproportionate number of violent criminals. In the study of collective human behaviour, however, neither laboratory experiments with the limbic system nor controlled genetic selection are significant. The human race is not a laboratory species nor do its members obey genetically selective rules in yielding to sexual attraction. It is, thank goodness, still love that makes the world go round.

If hard science will not show us the origins of war, we must look elsewhere, to the softer world of social science, and particularly to anthropology and psychology. One of the earliest general explanations of group aggression was proposed by Sigmund Freud in 1913, who considered the patriarchal family was the most significant unit of society. He suggested that sons resented their father's sexual monopoly over the family's women and that this led to conflict, and eventually to the father's murder. The son's consequent guilt created revulsion against incest, and drove men first to take sexual partners only from beyond the family group and then to a primitive warfare of wife-stealing.

Now, it is certainly true that wife-stealing was a common cause of fighting among primitive peoples, particularly those which practised female infanticide as a means of limiting population increase. What is certainly also true, however, is that some such peoples, historically the Eskimo, for example, were notable for not waging war in any form we would recognise. Freud's theory, though attractive to those who shared his belief that our sexual natures dominate our behaviour, must be recognised as no better than guesswork.

Ethologists, who seek to establish how human beings develop and perpetuate behaviour patterns, work by guesswork also, though at least from the basis of observed animal behaviour. In 1966 the most famous ethologist of aggression, Konrad Lorenz, a Nobel prizewinner, published his theory of territoriality. Predatory animals, he argued, have hunting territories, which they defend, but also submissive reflexes that deter them from attacking interlopers stronger than themselves. However when Man the Hunter invented weapons, he learnt to kill at a distance beyond the range at which submissive reflexes work. When territory was hunted out, he then began to fight other men over territorial rights.

The idea of territoriality was refined by Robert Ardrey, who added the observation that hunting, but also fighting, yields larger kills to individuals who co-operate in groups. His explanation of the origins of the hunting band, was enlarged by the improbably named Robin Fox and Lionel Tiger. They argued that the presence of females in such bands distracted from their main purpose, so they became all-male. The most effective and by implication most aggressive hunter emerged as the leader and, since he effectively ensured the livelihood of the band and all its dependants, male and female, aggressive male leadership thereafter determined the ethos of every human society.

Society, in short, like it or not, is red in tooth and claw. Many students of society, particularly in the world of anthropology, did not like the idea at all. Long before the ethologists entered the field, others attempted to translate Darwin's theory of natural selection from the animal to the human kingdom. The opponents of Social Darwinism, as it came to be known, protested that man's capacity to choose liberated him from the necessity to dominate or defer, to kill or be killed.

Perhaps the most celebrated of anti-Darwinians is the American Margaret Mead. As a young anthropologist in the 1920s, she returned from the South Seas with the news that she had discovered in Samoa an ideal society, a society in which patriarchal authority was dissolved within the affections of the extended family, free love had abolished sexual jealousy, children did not compete and violence was almost unknown. Samoans lived as they did, she said, because they chose to do so – and she argued that what they chose, others could. Much attacked by moralists in her time, and now criticised by fellow anthropologists for defective methodology, she never faltered in her permissive beliefs. She remained a dedicated anti-militarist and, in 1940, restated her faith in human free will in a now famous article, 'War is only an Invention – Not a Biological Necessity'.

The proposition that war may indeed be only an invention has driven a new generation of anthropologists to examine as many primordial societies as still remain, particularly those in the South American rain forest and highland New Guinea, for evidence of how they make war or why they do not.

The range of behaviour discovered is very wide, from the very violent indeed, as among the Yanomamö of Brazil, to the almost wholly pacific, as among the Semai of Malaysia. The military practices of these peoples are of the highest intrinsic interest, particularly the practice of ritual or symbolic combat, by which conflict is resolved with little killing, sometimes without bloodletting at all. Such restraint, where found, lends support to the view that our ancestors were not as violent as we, that war is not in our genes and that we may indeed, by choice, revert to wiser ways.

Unfortunately, there is no certainty at all that the surviving primitives are primordial or that their ways of war represent those of our ancestors of the main stream. The prevailing anthropological consensus is that the peoples of distant forests and mountains are simply the losers in a long-drawn-out process of adaptation. They have been, in the language of anthropology, 'marginalised' in the competition to inhabit land of first choice, and we must therefore regard the quaint military habits of those who avoid bloody battle as a reflection of their failure as warriors, not as evidence of a lost social wisdom.

I have to say I myself accept the implications of the theory of marginalisation with reluctance. War may have got worse with the passage of time, but the ethic of restraint has rarely been wholly absent from its practice. We know, of course, of episodes in which the victors killed without mercy. We know equally that even in the age of total warfare, there remain taboos, enshrined in law and thankfully widely observed, against killing the defenceless, women, children, the old, the sick and wounded, and those who care for them. I cannot believe that these inhibitions do not have very deep roots in human nature and am convinced that the symbolic and ritual military customs of the surviving primitives are significant to our understanding of war.

Nevertheless, we must recognise that at some moment combat became nakedly purposeful. When was that? Not long ago in the very long timescale of human existence. If we date the present phase of our life on earth from the latest retreat of the glaciers, we divide the subsequent twelve thousand years into a short period when man could still subsist as a hunter and the later, longer period when he had to find some other means of livelihood.

It is an illusion to believe that pesticides and herbicides have been the principal destroyers of wildlife. It was hunting that killed off the great herds and large-bodied animals in the temperate regions, and with such efficiency that man was driven first to protecting the survivors in domesticated flocks and then to cultivating the vegetable life on which they subsisted for his own consumption. Yet pastoralism and agriculture are not, as we congratulate ourselves, self-evident advances for human beings. Their development marks both a desperate necessity and a regression. The life of a nomad was probably healthier by far than that of the farmer, happier too, and as long as wildlife remained plentiful, more prosperous also.

Perhaps more pacific as well; hunting bands may have been driven to fight each other over territory as herds dwindled but, since many major species – the horse in North America, for example – were wiped out long before the available territory was fully populated, it seems more probable that the hunters would have migrated to find fresh prey rather than stay to squabble over the depleted hunting grounds. Certainly the evidence for the practice of warfare among late Stone Age hunters is even more sparse than their numbers were and too ambiguous to be argued convincingly either way.

The appearance in the temperate world, ten thousand years ago, of agricultural communities in the river valleys and near other water sources must, however, have confronted the hunting societies with a novel and tempting opportunity. Hunters, used to a diet of flesh, may not have been attracted initially by the farmer's stored grain crops; but their sheep and cattle must have looked easy meat. We may infer that from the very early appearance of fixed defences at the first agricultural sites. At Jericho, in modern Israel, for example, archaeology has revealed that the community settled around the perpetual spring in the desert had built a circular wall, dug a moat and erected a tower to protect their little city as early as 8000 BC. Only the threat of violence by raiders from the arid zone beyond can have prompted them to undertake such an expensive and time-consuming labour.

Other communities, in Egypt and Mesopotamia, enjoyed an easier start in agriculture. The Egyptians of the Nile Valley, surrounded by deep desert on either side and protected by the delta to the north and cataracts to the south, appear not to have faced a military challenge until about 2000 BC. As a result, their civilisation was dominated at the outset not by warriors but by priests whose authority derived from their power, as it was believed, to intervene with the gods who regulated the annual flood.

Civilisation in Mesopotamia, the land between the Tigris and Euphrates rivers in modern Iraq, was originally also theocratic, the function of its priest-kings being that of organising the distribution of the annual floodwater into irrigation channels. Mesopotamia's natural defences, however, are weaker than Egypt's, more easily penetrated by raiders from the desert and the nearby mountains, while the distribution of the yearly snow-melt, more lethargic by far than the Nile's overflowing, in itself entailed dispute and the regulation of conflict.

It is understandable, therefore, that, while the archaeology of Egypt tells us of a kingdom long peaceful, that of Mesopotamia exhibits the development of a military system as early as 3000 BC – in writing, in fortification and also in the appearance of metallic armour and weapons. The small cities of the flood plain were then evidently fighting among themselves, how regularly we do not know. It is apparent, however, that conflict was leading to consolidation, that centres of power were amalgamating, that weapon systems – particularly the horse-drawn chariot – were under development and that the military culture of the Mesopotamians was beginning to embrace the idea of offensive warfare.

The saga of Gilgamesh, ruler of the city of Uruk, tells in one of the earliest documents of history, written about 2700 BC, the story of what is unmistakably an offensive military campaign. Only a thousand years later, about 1300 BC, a successor kingdom of Uruk, that of Assur or Assyria, had become a true military empire. The Assyrians had now passed beyond the stage of beating back the savage raiders of the deserts and mountains from their borders, were carrying the attack to their enemies, and had created the first recognisable army in history – made up of specialists of several sorts, engineers, and logistic troops as well as charioteers and infantrymen.

The origins of war had been surpassed. War was now a fact of life and a chief function of another new fact of life, the state. What is the relationship between war and the state? Must states make war? It is that question my next lecture addresses.

CHAPTER THREE
WAR AND THE STATE

'WAR MADE THE STATE AND THE STATE MAKES WAR'
goes an academic jingle, familiar to most students of
political science. The first half of the jingle would not
excite argument among lay people, who would sensibly
say that the origins of the state are lost in the mists of
time. The second half – that, by implication, the principal function of the state is to make war – would arouse
surprise and probably protest. In my previous lectures
I surveyed the origins of war and traced how the evolution of conflict is linked to the evolution of social
groupings and the development of the nation state.
Tonight I shall explore the role of the state in more
detail.

Paradoxically, the state known to modern Western
Europeans and North Americans is a benevolent, not a
belligerent institution. It educates, heals and feeds,
through the institutions of the school and university
system, the health services and social security provi-
sion, and does much else besides. It is a giving, not a
taking entity, in marked contrast to many nineteenth-
century states, which were known to citizens chiefly for

taking their sons to serve in the army. Today's nation state *is* a welfare state, and not much more besides.

If the functions of the state are at all a cause of difference between citizens today, it is because they disagree over how much the state should give. To give, it must take, of course, and all taxpayers groan at fiscal deductions from what they earn. The right of the state to tax is now contested, however, only by a handful of extreme libertarians. Taxation is accepted by the vast majority as necessary to the collective good. It is only the question of whether state spending affects for the bad the individual virtues of independence, self-sufficiency and choice that arouses dispute.

The nannying by the nanny state of the old, sick and very poor carries consent; that of those suspected of having brought misfortune upon themselves often does not. The dispute translates sometimes onto the moral plane: should the state usurp the individual's right to choose? Should the fiscal system not be so arranged that the citizen is left sufficient financial freedom to decide what school his children attend, what doctor he consults, what pension he buys?

At either level of debate, the issue is, nevertheless, about how much the state should or should not provide. The idea that the state itself should be provided with services by the citizen, the even starker idea that it should take without giving at all, simply does not arise. And yet until very recent times the state gave little more than quite sketchy services of domestic law and order while, at times, taking very much indeed. In 1793 the French Republic instituted decrees which required every citizen to put himself or herself at the state's disposition, the decree most strictly enforced that requiring every young man to serve in the army.

Where the French Republic led, other states followed, with the result that by the nineteenth century's end most European states had taken draconian powers to extract service from their younger male citizens and were in consequence potent war-making agencies and, it might be thought, very little else besides.

That phase in the history of the state, at least the liberal democratic state, has passed. Since 1945 there has been a progressive abandonment of the state's demand for universal military service, a trend accelerated since the fall of the Berlin Wall in 1989. The United States and Britain were by then already relying on quite small volunteer forces for their defence and their example is becoming general.

France has announced that it will abolish conscription within the next decade, an extraordinary decision for a country which invented the practice in its modern form and long insisted that only by doing uniformed duty to the Republic could its young be taught civic virtue. Germany insists that conscription must continue, because citizen enlistment guarantees that its armed forces will remain dutiful to democracy.

This judgement, superficially, is understandable in terms of Germany's history – its generosity in granting the right of conscientious objection means, neverthe-less, that service is in effect voluntary. Even Russia, which has maintained vast conscript armies for cen-turies, is now talking of moving to a voluntary system. All over Europe and the Americas, armies are withering away. Only in Asia and Africa do large armed forces continue in existence, often as the instruments of self-ishly dictatorial regimes. Wherever electorates rule, most are withdrawing their consent from the state's right to make their sons soldiers.

This development offers not only a striking new dimension to the debate over whether it is the state's principal role to make war. It also calls into question the logic of the proposition that the state and the prac-tice of warmaking are entangled in an inextricable and unique relationship. The modern liberal democratic state exerts powers and accepts responsibilities greater by far than those given to and laid on its predecessors. If it now subordinates its military functions to those of providing for the welfare, education, health care and often housing of its citizens, ought we not to re-exam-ine the historical record to identify whether warmaking has always predominated among the state's activities?

Equally, many of the hundred and fifty states that have come into existence since 1945, when there were only fifty sovereignties, display a fierce capacity to make war but otherwise perform almost none of the duties expected of a state. They deserve, in short, the description of state only because they are warlike. Since many modern wars are not conducted by states at all, ought we not to re-examine the idea that it is war-making that defines the states?

History does provide grounds for disbelieving in the inevitable destiny of states to fight. The Egyptian river kingdom of the first pharaohs, to take a notable example, may have been, probably was, unified by force. Once unified, however, it enjoyed a period of undisturbed peace for nearly fifteen hundred years, from 3000 to 1700 BC. There were special geographical reasons for that. It was too isolated to be easily attacked and, because of the wealth that the Nile flood brought, had no material reason to attack others.

It might, nevertheless, have settled for a hand-to-mouth way of economic life at subsistence level, as other ecologically favoured societies often did, notably in the islands of Polynesia. That proved not to be the Egyptians' choice. Under the rule of the god-kings, they found ways of avoiding the Polynesian pattern of cyclical expulsion of surplus population by violence, devising means instead to intensify agricultural yield. Meanwhile the energy that might have been consumed in domestic warmaking was diverted instead into the creation of great works of monumental art, rivalling, perhaps exceeding in grandeur, all other artistic achievements of Mediterranean antiquity and still a wonder of the world.

The life of the common Egyptian under pharaonic rule might not have suited you or me. Theirs was clearly not a free society nor one where the individual, however rich or important, counted for much under the hierarchy of the gods. Pharaonic Egypt was, nevertheless, that politically scientific contradiction in terms, a true state, working at the highest level of cultural activity, which found no need to wage war for a period as long as Europe has been Christian. Only when Nubian raiders started to penetrate the upper Nile valley – in about 1900 BC – did the kingdom begin to add fortification to its architectural activity. Foreigners who had acquired the new technology of the war chariot only appeared on the lower Nile from 1600 BC, when the pharaohs finally had to become war leaders.

So a state without a military culture, without even a standing army, is a perfectly practical polity. Does the contradiction work the other way round? Can there be an army without a state? All too easily, if the history of the horse peoples of the Central Asian steppe is taken into account. Until about four thousand years ago, the horse was kept chiefly for eating. Then, either through mutation or selective breeding, a variety of horse appeared that was strong enough to be used to pull a vehicle and, soon after, to be ridden by a man. The military value of the domesticated horse was quickly grasped. Chariot-driving warrior aristocracies seized power all over the Middle East, China and Mediterranean Europe during the second millennium BC and held it until the nearly simultaneous appearance of iron weapons and ridden cavalry horses toppled their bronze-based monopoly of military force about 1000 BC.

Then other developments, notably those of standing armies in Europe and strategic fortification in China, beat the horse warriors back onto the steppe, where the domesticated horse probably originated, and there they stayed for over a thousand years. They made their first reappearance in Western history when Attila's Huns attacked the Roman Empire in the fifth century AD and returned in successive waves throughout the early middle ages, but as a nagging threat rather than a destructive menace. In the thirteenth century, however, a thitherto unknown horse people, Genghis Khan's Mongols, emerged from the great Central Asian sea of grass to fall on settled civilisation in the greatest campaign of conquest ever known. Within a single century Genghis and his descendants had overthrown the power of the Islamic Caliphate and the Chinese throne, to control an empire which stretched from the Pacific to the Black Sea, from Siberia to the Himalayas, from the Persian Gulf to the Sea of Japan.

Historians of the Mongol conquests make much of the Mongols' military sophistication and of their skills in subordinating conquered peoples to their power. They were indeed adept at perpetuating the administrative systems they found in place and in enforcing order. To argue hence that the Mongols were a political people and their empire a state seems to me to defy meaning. Mongol conquest had a single purpose – to extract, by violent extortion, the revenue that would allow them to enjoy, in luxury rather than poverty, their nomadic and warrior way of life.

So determined were they to remain horse warriors that, in China, large areas of agricultural land were turned back into pasture for the grazing herds and the dispossessed peasants massacred. Genghis himself said that the greatest pleasure in life was to 'chase and defeat the enemy, seize his possessions, ride his horse, leave his married women weeping and use their bodies as a nightshirt'.* It is not surprising, in view of Genghis's world outlook, that there are no biographies of Mongol scholars, thinkers, artists or entrepreneurs or that, though they were in their time the most powerful people in the world, no political, cultural or intellectual achievement can be associated with their rule whatsoever. Their society found no place for any man who was not a warrior and they ended, as they began, an army on horseback.

If we can accept that history yields examples both of states without armies and armies detached from states, we can return with a fresh eye to the proposition that war is exclusively a state activity and that states are necessarily warmaking agencies. The first part of the proposition can be dismissed with confidence. War is clearly not an exclusively state activity, was not in the past and is not in the present, as the rise of non-state warfare, in

---

*Paul Ratchnevsky, *Genghis Khan* (Blackwell, 1991, p. 153).

the Balkans, for example, painfully exemplifies.

The second part of the proposition is more contentious. The state must clearly maintain internal peace as a minimum condition of its acceptability to those who live under its authority. It must, equally, secure its borders against external attack for the same reason. Do those two responsibilities therefore define it as an essentially military entity?

The states that dominate the history books – those of classical Greece, the Roman Republic and its successors, the Islamic Caliphate, the Chinese empire – were clearly very military indeed. The Greek city states and the later Roman Republic and Empire accepted war as a condition of survival and waged it very fiercely. Chinese civilisation deprecated warmaking, however, from early times – one of the best-known of Confucian aphorisms teaches that 'the rational man achieves his ends without violence' – while the rise of the great monotheistic religions of Christianity and Islam caused the European and Near Eastern peoples that embraced them to agonise over the morality of killing fellow children of God for centuries.

Islam, a religion much misunderstood in the West, was a conquering creed in origin. Its holy book forbids, nevertheless, the use of violence against those who submit, so that non-believers who yield to Islamic authority must be granted both the freedom to practise their own religion and protection against their enemies.

Many early Christians interpreted the New

Testament as a pacifist text and, though the early Christian powers believed otherwise in practice, the idea that the Ten Commandments should regulate relations at least between Christian peoples was translated into a set of elaborate legal codes.

These required the doing of penance for shedding Christian blood – forty days' penance for even wounding a fellow Christian, done by the Norman knights after the victory of Hastings – and the avoidance of warmaking during the Christian year's penitential seasons, Advent and Lent. Islam went further. The Prophet's prohibition of fighting between Muslims was taken so seriously by the devout that, during the civil wars of the early Caliphate, contestants recruited armies of infidel slaves to do the fighting on their behalf.

As long as states deferred to superordinate authority, to priests and the religion they preached, they could avoid confronting the moral dilemma in which their use of violence involved them. Since worldly power came from God, and his priests taught how it might and might not be used, states, or at least their leaders, did not have to take a view about whether the use of violence was intrinsic to their status. Religion and its rules removed the matter, as it were, from their hands, leaving legitimate states in a morally subordinate position. All that was changed, at least in Western Europe, by the division of Christianity at the Reformation, when religious authority itself became the cause of conflict. The Protestant states thereafter rejected the right of the Universal Church to judge their actions, while the Catholic states took that rejection as grounds to make war against them in clear conscience.

The outcome was the Thirty Years War, the worst thus far in European history, which may have killed a third of the German-speaking peoples and left Central Europe devastated for much of the seventeenth century. Those awful results of the collapse of universal and superordinate authority provoked the search for an alternative legal basis on which relationships between the states could be established. It was found by a new profession of international jurists, who proposed that, since states could no longer agree on where higher sovereignty lay, they should each become sovereign themselves. As sovereignties, they would exist as independent moral entities, perhaps better amoral entities, each judging how it should behave, exclusively in terms of its own interests.

From the idea of the amorally sovereign state – anticipated by Machiavelli at the beginning of the Renaissance – to that of the state as a purposefully and perhaps primarily warmaking machine was but a short step. Europe was set a bad example by the First French Republic, which claimed justification for its widespread aggression in its self-assumed duty to bring the rights of liberty and equality to oppressed peoples elsewhere.

The success with which it waged ideological war prompted the Prussian soldier, Carl von Clausewitz, to promulgate the most pernicious philosophy of warmaking yet conceived. War, he said, is nothing more than the continuation of politics by means of force – he may have meant policy, the German word *Politik* obscures the point – and it is to be limited only by the calculation of the political interest in which it was undertaken in the first place.

War, in short, is a value-free activity, outside the moral sphere; but the implication is that politics is too, since the state's use of force works in a continuum that begins with the punishment of its own citizens who defy its interests. Therefore nothing can or should restrain the state's right to act violently except the threat of superior violence in return.

I call Clausewitz pernicious because his political philosophy underlies that of the totalitarian state. It is significant that his is the only name mentioned in Hitler's political testament, written just before he killed himself in the Berlin Bunker, amid the ruins of the state he had led to destruction, in April, 1945. By then historical fact had twice denied the Clausewitzian dictum that war limits itself rationally, if not morally, by the automatic operation of calculation of state interest.

The First World War quite escaped the control of Germany's rulers in 1918, leaving them unable to negotiate a way out of national starvation except by compete capitulation to all the victor's demands. By 1945, Hitler's refusal, as head of state, to negotiate in the state's interests in any way led to the extinction of sovereignty itself, while his completely amoral use of state power in the prosecution of the war condemned his people to pariah status among nations for decades afterwards.

Even while Clausewitz was polluting civilised thought about how wars could and should be fought, other and contrary influences were at work. In reaction to the military excesses of the French Revolution and the Napoleonic empire, the chief European states attempted, after 1815, to create a continental system that would avert war between its members by subordinating sovereignty to the commonly shared value of preserving peace. It worked for nearly fifty years. The resurgence of warmaking towards the century's end was not accepted with complacency. The international Hague Convention of 1899 had as its object, accepted by the signatories, not only the limitation of armaments but the creation of a supranational court, designed to avert war by arbitration. There was a second Hague Convention in 1907, while a third was planned for 1915.

By then the reasonable Hague system had been overwhelmed by the worst European war since that of the Thirty Years. Its spirit, however, survived. After 1918 jurists returned to the issue of how relations between states should be regulated. While their predecessors after 1648 had elevated state sovereignty to a supreme position, untrammelled sovereignty was now itself identified as the enemy of peace. Even before the war's end, President Wilson of the United States had proposed the creation of a League of Nations which would exercise the superordinate authority lost at the Reformation – and in 1928, a Franco-American pact to which many nations subscribed renounced the use of war 'as an instrument of policy'.

In 1939 Hitler made a mockery both of the League of Nations and the Kellogg-Briand Pact. Neither, however, would lie down. In 1945 there was brought into being an Organisation of United Nations which established, by charter and consent, both the subordination of all military sovereignty to its own and the illegality of war itself, self-defence excepted, unless sanctioned by its own authority.

The world, in consequence, has now returned to the international system that arose when states first began to acknowledge the superior authority of monotheistic religion. States are no longer militarily sovereign any more than those within the European Union are politically sovereign, even if that Union did not, as its most enthusiastic supporters claim, originate as an anti-war association. States are subordinate to a power greater than themselves. They cannot make war at wish, certainly cannot claim state interest or political necessity to make war as they choose.

The ordinary citizen who doubts that it is the state's chief role to make war on his behalf has, even if over a very long timespan, been proved right after all. How that legacy has shaped his life as an individual will be the subject of my next lecture.

Chapter Four
War and the Individual

'EVERY MAN,' SAID DOCTOR JOHNSON, 'thinks meanly of himself for not having been a soldier or not having been at sea.' His thought is often misquoted as 'every man thinks better of himself for having been a soldier'. Either way, we know what he meant. It is the rare man who does not think better of himself for having served, in whatever capacity, and even if he had not faced gunfire. To have worn uniform, to have done drill, to have submitted to the discipline of a military community enlarges, particularly in retrospect, and more amply as time passes, a man's opinion of himself.

That is particularly so in Britain, where the ethos of the squadron, the ship's company and, above all, the small regimental community is strong. The reunions of those who fought in the Second World War have attracted larger numbers even as the war has grown more distant. The fiftieth anniversaries of the D-Day invasion that liberated Europe, and of the culminating peace of 1945, brought record turnouts. They also brought the cheers of the multitude and the private congratulations of family and friends. Old soldiers and sailors and airmen were indeed caused to think better of themselves, often by members of a generation which has no memory of the war at all.

So far, in previous lectures, I have explored the origins of war, and the changing role of the state in its prosecution. Yet the role of individuals in warfare, and the impact of war upon them, deserve greater attention and it is to them that I turn in this fourth lecture. There are special reasons for the high standing in which veterans are held in Britain. They are the men and women who first averted defeat – how close did defeat loom in 1940 – and then brought total victory over a monstrous tyranny. It was a victory, moreover, not won at the wicked cost in lives of the First World War. The losses were grievous enough, nearly four hundred thousand deaths in battle, but fewer by nearly half than those of 1914–18.

The grief of the bereaved, moreover, was alleviated by the value of the sacrifice. 'They did not die in vain' is, for once, a form of words not empty of meaning, while the extraordinarily gracious way the British have found of commemorating each individual who died, in the mysteriously beautiful war cemeteries maintained around the globe, is in itself a comfort to the nations' widows and orphans. The Russians, who lost ten million in battle, have no such comfort. The reunions of their veterans are still haunted by men and women seeking any scrap of news of sons or husbands who disappeared without trace at Stalingrad or Kursk fifty

years ago. The lot of the Germans of the war generation, however little sympathy they deserve, is worse by
far. Stalin ordered the systematic destruction of every
German war grave on Soviet soil, where most of
Germany's four million lost soldiers fell, while those
who survived rarely find reason for reunion. They have
nothing to celebrate and much, including dishonour, to
forget.

Yet even the old men who were Hitler's soldiers
escape individual dishonour. They were patriotic in
their time, and are honoured for that by their country-
men, and they were usually brave, as their enemies
freely admit. They benefit from the indulgence granted
by the human heart to all young men of the twentieth
century whom the state plucked from peaceful life, put
into uniform and sent to do an often fatal duty. The
idea of the common soldier, of whatever country, of
whatever war, as victim is strong in our culture, and
with reason. War has, in our time, chosen many victims
but none so numerous as the ordinary soldier himself.

The idea of the soldier as victim would have been
quite alien to many of our ancestors for much of
history. They would simply not have understood what
grounds Doctor Johnson thought the military or naval
life gave to men for thinking better of themselves. He,
we may guess, conceived the soldier or sailor – and he
probably meant officers in any case – to be an individual who voluntarily accepted the risk of death as a
duty within a strictly disciplined service. The redcoat

army, the bluejacket navy of the eighteenth century flogged and hanged without mercy when its code was broken, and the breaches of law it punished with violence included rape and looting as well as mutiny. To the inhabitants of the Spanish Netherlands during the Eighty Years War, to the inhabitants of Germany in the Thirty Years War, to the inhabitants of France during the Hundred Years War, rape and looting were what the approach of an army portended.

The soldier was a hated figure in mediaeval and renaissance Europe, as the paintings of Breughel and the engravings of Callot graphically portray. A despised one also: soldiers ate and drank at the common people's expense, uncontrolled by their officers; they were a roughriding lot themselves who also took what they chose, including sexual favours, paid for nothing and, if opposed, tortured and killed. When the common people got their chance of revenge, they took it. Callot's series of engravings divides equally into scenes of atrocity by soldiers against civilians and of reprisals by civilians against soldiers when stragglers fell into their clutches. The image of the soldier as criminal or oppressor belongs, moreover, to most times and places. The Roman soldiers of the New Testament – men under authority, as Christ's dialogue with the centurion reminds us – supplied not merely his torturers and executioners but, if St Paul's appeal to soldiers not to commit extortion conveys anything about their behaviour, they were blackmailers and robbers as well.

Why, for so long and in so many places, was the individual soldier hated and despised? Hated because he misbehaved, of course; despised because he was usually a person plucked from the lowest ranks of society, a man unable to make an honest living or someone who put himself beyond the bounds of honesty, by fathering an illegitimate child he could not support, by committing theft or murder. Enlistment offered him an escape from the law, armies being unfussy about accepting recruits who were usefully brutal, as long as they would thereafter submit to the brutal rules of obedience armies themselves imposed. The soldier was regarded as a being particularly low in the sophisticated society of China, where his status equated with that of prostitutes and criminals.

Even in Victorian Britain, which tolerated no civil misbehaviour by Tommy Atkins, the common soldier was a social outcast. Since he was forbidden to marry without permission and in any case earned too little to support a wife, he could not belong to respectable society. 'I would rather see you buried than in a red coat' wrote the mother of William Robertson, a future field-marshal, when he gave up a position as a domestic servant to go for a soldier.* Better a footman than a cavalryman, her honest village soul protested, even in an age when the Widow of Windsor's army was run as strictly as a Sunday School.

*Victor Bonham-Carter, *Soldier True* (Muller, 1963, p. 5).

How, then, had Doctor Johnson taken the view that men could think better of themselves for having been a soldier? It is not too difficult to solve the conundrum. The possession of superior force is a perpetual temptation to behave badly, and we lack no evidence of that from our newspapers and television screens. The strong sometimes kill the weak as if by a rule of human nature and can actually be stimulated to kill by the victim's weakness. My friend Don McCullin, the great war photographer, a witness of terrible scenes of massacre in Lebanon and elsewhere, gives it as his opinion that the attempt to reason with armed men bent on murder positively discourages them from feeling pity.

There is, however, a contrary principle in human nature, one which we also recognise as an apparently universal rule. That is that the use of force by the strong against the weak is an intrinsically repellent activity. Typically, it brings remorse; we define the psychopath as a being incapable of remorse. Equally typically, the desire to avoid the occasion of remorse translates, both in the individual and in the culture to which he belongs, into the ethic of fair fight. Sport supplies an analogy. Winning teams take no satisfaction in defeating known losers. They seek a contest between equals, glory in victory if they achieve it, acquiesce in honourable defeat if they do not.

It is the idea of military honour that explains Dr Johnson's judgement. The pursuit of honour in battle has very ancient origins, not unnaturally, for they lie deep in the human psyche. Even in the comparatively bloodless ritual battles of primitives, young men competed to be seen taking risk. In more complex societies, the pursuit of risk becomes entangled with that of social standing itself, in two directions. Successful warriors acquire superior weapons. So equipped, they seek to do battle only with those similarly armed. In Bronze Age China, charioteers, we are told, despised fighting common foot soldiers, choosing to pit themselves if possible against enemy charioteers alone.

The *Iliad*, the most influential story of war in Western literature, is almost exclusively about honour. Not only do the Greeks go to Troy on a matter of honour. Once arrived, their champions are spurred to fight the Trojan champions as much for honour as for victory itself.

The Homeric ideal has permeated Western history. One of Alexander the Great's first acts on invading Persia in 334 BC was to take from a temple armour allegedly worn at Troy, allegedly by Greeks whom he claimed as ancestors, while, two millennia later, the thought that they would disembark within sight of Troy inspired many young classical scholars among the officers of the expeditionary force that sailed to Gallipoli.

Yet the Homeric ideal of honour would seem gravely defective to the modern professional soldier, indeed to his knightly and aristocratic predecessors. The victor in the Homeric duel showed no respect whatsoever for his vanquished foe. The passage in which Achilles exults as he drags the body of the fallen Hector behind his chariot is perhaps the most horrifying in the horrific story of the *Iliad*. Honour could be savage, as the reports by Christian missionaries of the tests of courage inflicted by the North American Indians on their proud captives all too vividly portray. It was only when the practice of honour came to be palliated by a higher moral code, particularly that of Christianity itself, that the warrior learned to honour his enemy even in defeat.

Chivalry began, quite late in the history of Christian Europe, as a code for the rich alone. Because it was so heavily mythologised, as much in the nineteenth as the fourteenth century, it is now much doubted if it was ever a governing ethic at all. Yet it undoubtedly was, and it undoubtedly came eventually to influence the behaviour in battle of the poor warrior as much as it did that of his social superior. The rules requiring decent treatment of all prisoners, irrespective of rank, for example, were already widely observed by professional armies in the eighteenth century; what outraged European officers of both sides during the Franco-British wars in North America was that the allied Indians tortured captured common soldiers, though not officers, in flagrant violation of what were by then civilised standards.

By the late nineteenth century, much, though by no means exclusively, influenced by the humanitarian

Geneva Conventions, European armies enforced elaborate codes of correct behaviour, which were accepted as a matter of course by the rank and file. Not only European armies: the foreign observers with the Japanese army in the Russo-Japanese war of 1904-5 reported very favourably on the conduct of the ordinary Japanese soldier, towards both the enemy and Manchurian civilians.

The Samurai class, which officered Japan's new Western-style army, had imposed its own knightly code of honour on the peasant recruits. It was only in the 1930s, when fanatically nationalist officers took charge, that the Japanese armed forces began deliberately to brutalise recruits in training, with the object of filling them with hate that would then be turned on foreigners. Tens of thousands of Allied prisoners-of-war suffered the consequences; so did millions of Chinese civilians.

I spoke in an earlier lecture of the militarisation of Europe in the nineteenth century. That was an undoubted fact of the continent's development, as it was of Japan's westernisation. The product was the vast armies that marched to war in 1914, armies disciplined for battle but also in a code of decent military behaviour. The code worked. Apart from an early and short passage of deliberate 'frightfulness' by the Germans in Belgium, the armies of the Great War did not commit atrocities, either against each other or against civilians. They did not rape, nor loot, nor mistreat wounded or prisoners, nor behave in any way at all as both the Catholic and Protestant armies had done in Germany during the Thirty Years War.

What we know of our own British Expeditionary Force helps to explain why. The code by then had sunk civilian as well as military roots. The volunteer battalions that went off to die on the Somme in 1916, under the half-comic names they had chosen for themselves – 'Church Lads', 'Glasgow Tramways', 'Accrington Pals', '1st Football' – were the creations not only of a surge of patriotic emotion, but also of Victorian respectability and all its agencies, church, chapel, workplace, close-knit industrial town and athletic fraternity.

It is odd to reflect, but true nonetheless, that the British working-class men who went off to the Great War had quite unselfconsciously chosen as their boyhood leisure reading, if not the *Boy's Own Paper*, perhaps too expensive for their pockets, then something quite like it, something suffused with the idea of fair play, the honour of the school, doing the decent thing and standing up for the weak and the weaker sex. The regular officers who commanded them had no need to teach the code of honour they had learnt at their public schools and at Woolwich and Sandhurst. It was already implanted in the volunteers' breasts. Equivalent codes possessed the armies of France, Germany, Austria-Hungary and Russia, even if in a more institutionally religious than secular form. It was the idea of honour, and its associated ideals of duty and self-sacrifice, that supplied the energy of the First World War.

With what terrible effect; earlier and different societies recognised the implausibility of the attempt to make every man a soldier, as Europe tried to do in 1914 and again in 1939. Primitive societies may have expected all males to be warriors; most, the exceptional 'hard' primitives excepted, took care to wage war in a way that did not try their warriors too hard. Historically, developed societies have recognised that the life of the soldier is not for the many. It requires qualities not only of physical strength and endurance but of emotional robustness found only in the few.

Rich commercial societies, in consequence, often hired mercenaries or regulars to do their fighting for them. Islam, by origin the most militant of polities, eventually went to the edge of the Steppe to buy hard nomads to defend its borders. The Tsars enlisted their surplus serfs. Frederick the Great kidnapped to man his armies. George III rented armies intact from the smaller German states to fight his rebellious American subjects. Only in recent times, only really in the twentieth century, have states reverted to the practice of the Greek cities and obliged all male citizens to go to war. Many proved quite unsuited to the responsibility.

Why was that? Because of the duration of modern wars, for one thing. It may surprise many, although it should not have really been forgotten, that Greek wars were very short, a day of battle at most, and the battles were short too – an hour of killing in which one side or the other was broken, the losers fled home and the victors buried the dead. The great twentieth-century wars lasted for years, and battles for month after month. Verdun, usually cited as the worst battle of the twentieth century, lasted from February to November 1916, and many French soldiers were ordered to the battlefront several times over.

Those who survived repeated exposure to wounds or death – and two out of nine French soldiers who went to the war were killed – passed through successive moods of resignation, fatalism and eventual despair. In the spring of 1917, when the number of French deaths in action equalled that of the strength of the French army on mobilisation, the army's resolution broke. Over half of its divisions joined a military strike, the men announcing their unwillingness to attack again; there were similar breakdowns of morale in the Italian and Russian armies later in the year and in the German army in 1918, all of which had suffered comparable casualties.

The protraction of war had, in short, undermined the individual's essential belief in the statistical probability of his own survival, the calculation that 'it won't be me'. At the same time, the experience of the individual as long as he survived was nastier than ever before – measured in terms of noise, general insecurity and the spectacle of the wounds inflicted by modern weapons, including burns and multiple fragmentation effects. War had got longer. It had also got worse. The outcome was a rising incidence of psychological casualties, a phenomenon largely denied during the First World War but necessarily recognised during the Second.

We must re-phrase Dr Johnson: 'Every man would think better of himself for having been a soldier, could he bear the strain.' Large minorities of mass armies, it has been revealed in our time, cannot. Individuals crack under fear, sometimes the anticipation of fear, and so do whole units, particularly those formed of an army's second or third choice of personnel. The recent trend for the armed forces of developed states to shed numbers reflects not only the economic difficulty of maintaining and equipping the totality of manpower available for service.

It also reflects their acceptance of the doubtful utility of large numbers themselves. In retrospect, I would argue that the function of the large armies of the First World War was chiefly to act as a medium through which the imposition of heavy casualties would inflict pain on the civilian populations that supported the war. I spoke in my first lecture of the telegraph boy on his bicycle, pedalling the suburban street, who became for parents and wives literally an omen of terror.

Even in the Second World War, when technological development and industrial expansion could equip more of the mass with weapons designed to counter enemy weapons, the role of many was simply to fill space as targets for the enemy's firepower. It is only in our own time that the pointlessness of opposing military machinery with men who lack such machinery has become fully apparent. It was demonstrated beyond argument in the Gulf War of 1991, when the mood possessing the pathetically under-equipped Iraqi army was to capitulate as soon as signs of surrender could be safely displayed.

War and the individual, we may recognise, are parting company. Only in unusual circumstances, remote both in place and time, was the relationship ever one for the majority. It is now a relationship, in the Western world at least, for a very small minority indeed. That minority remains critically important, both to our immediate wellbeing and to the world's future and in my final lecture I shall look ahead to the implications for the future of war.

While war has become far too expensive, financially and emotionally, for rich states to wage with anything approaching the full potentiality, technological and human, their resources make available, it has also become, paradoxically, a cheap and deadly undertaking for poor states, for enemies of the state idea, and for factions in states falling apart. The rogue ruler, the terrorist and the fundamentalist movement, the ethnic or religious faction are all enemies as serious as any, in an age of junk weapons, as civilisation has ever faced. The threat they offer requires that the responsible powers, committed to the maintenance of peace, must be able to deploy forces of the highest quality, human as well as technological, to any part of the globe at all times.

Membership of such forces require high skills. It also requires a particular ethic, a readiness by the individual to risk his – or her – life not simply for any of the traditional values by which warriors fought but for the cause of peace itself. The honour of the honourable warrior has acquired a new meaning. Its fulfilment will make all who perform it think better of themselves for having been a soldier. We must honour them also.

CHAPTER FIVE
CAN THERE BE AN END TO WAR?

'WE MUST KNOW,' WROTE HERACLITUS of Ephesus in the fifth century BC, 'that war is common to all and strife is justice, and that all things come into being and pass away through strife.'* His was a deeply classical view, formed by the relentless conflicts of the Greek world, both between Greek and Greek and against the power of the Persian empire. It was a view held by most free Greeks of his time, men who thought of themselves as warriors quite as much as they did as farmers, philosophers or historians and who took it for granted that they would, during the course of their lives, fight as spearmen in the phalanx or as sailors at sea.

Is this true today? Having considered in previous lectures the origins of war, and the changing role of individuals and states, in this final lecture I must address the outlook for the future. Can there ever be an end to war?

The classical idea of conflict as central to human life was to persist beyond the ancient world. Deprecated

*Quoted in Doyne Dawson, *The Origins of Western Warfare* (Westview Press, 1996, p. 11).

both by Christianity and Islam – the pious Muslim holds that the greater *jihad*, or holy war, is the war against self – it achieved a powerful revival in the nineteenth century, when science, through the work of Charles Darwin, moved to an interpretation of the life process itself as one of struggle within and between species. His theory of the natural selection of the fittest migrated into philosophy, the social sciences and politics, having its direst outcomes in various forms of socialism, particularly the Bolshevism of Lenin and the National Socialism of Adolf Hitler.

It is not surprising that, in the course of the modern world's rejection of communism and fascism, and all their works, Heraclitus's belief in the necessity of strife as a creative and corrective force has been rejected also. We live in an age that deprecates conflict and sets the ideals of harmony, compromise and communality above all others.

Communitarianism, a 'third way' between socialism and capitalism, is now the political movement that, under a variety of names and guises, most attracts democratic politicians. It commands also powerful support among electorates. 'We have had enough conflict in our century,' the ordinary voter seems to be saying. 'What we want is a way of life without strife.'

It would seem an attainable object, particularly to voters in this country. Britain has had a blessed half-century since 1945. After two terrible world wars, in the second of which we played a deeply honourable part, we have been spared almost every trouble that has afflicted so many of the world's other leading states in the aftermath. There may have been conflicts following our withdrawal from empire, but we managed the transition without provoking any war on a scale comparable to that fought by France in Algeria or Portugal in Africa. We avoided costly foreign strategic interventions, of the sort the United States made in Vietnam and Russia in Afghanistan.

Our only unilateral war, that in the Falklands, was both legal and victorious. Our participation in the Korean and Gulf wars was legal and laudable. We have made no serious enemies and kept many friends, while responsibly discharging onerous military duties, sanctioned by the United Nations, in scores of troublespots around the globe. The ordinary British citizen has good reasons for concluding that conflict in our time has been brought under control through wise diplomacy and the deployment of judiciously calculated force. Unluckier countries, less well-governed, less well-defended, have had different and unhappier experiences. Where we have shown the way, however, collective national opinion might argue, they can follow. Strife, the British would think, is not justice and war need certainly not be common at all.

These are comforting thoughts. They are also illusions. The central strategic fact with which we live, and with which our descendants must live for ever, is that of nuclear weapons. The development and use of nuclear weapons during the Second World War changed the way the world worked for good. Even before the First World War the international community may already have been groping its way towards a system within which international agreement would control the characteristics of weapons that might legally be used in war and any conflict threatening war would be submitted to supranational arbitration.

It was, however, only when the world was confronted in 1945 by a sort of weapon guaranteeing an unbearable excess of costs over benefits in any war in which it was used, that the absolute necessity of averting war between powers that possessed such weapons was grasped. That necessity remains and will persist.

Although it was the balance of terror throughout the Cold War which prevented nuclear war, can nuclear war be averted in perpetuity? I am optimistic. Man is a volatile and risk-taking species but a rational one also. In our relationship with nuclear weapons since 1945, it is rationality rather than volatility or risk-taking that has prevailed. There has been only one genuine nuclear crisis, that over the Russian deployment of nuclear missiles to Cuba in 1962, a crisis in any case resolved by reasonable negotiation. To set against that episode, we should recognise that, outside an atmosphere of crisis, there are many other negotiated settlements that have restricted the number of states permitted to possess nuclear weapons, the number of nuclear weapons that nuclear powers may themselves possess, the type of nuclear weapons that may be deployed in particular regions and the regions in which nuclear weapons may be deployed at all.

Space has been demilitarised by international agreement, so has Antarctica. Europe is a forbidden zone for the deployment of intermediate-range missiles. The United States and the former Soviet Union are bound by treaties that have reduced and aim to reduce still further the number of nuclear weapons. Most important of all, most of the world's sovereignties are signatories to a non-proliferation treaty that binds them not to become nuclear powers in perpetuity. The history of proliferation is in itself encouraging, particularly if an analogy is drawn with the rise of the last capital weapon system, the dreadnought battleship, at the beginning of the century. Between 1906 and 1914, eleven states followed Britain in becoming dreadnought powers, quite pointlessly in many cases. Between 1945 and 1960, only four states imitated America in acquiring nuclear weapons, and all adhere to the principle of non-proliferation, that is, that the number of nuclear states is now closed.

To pursue the optimistic note, we should also recognise the successes achieved in the limitation of non-nuclear weapons. Disarmament is a word that evokes a weary response, perhaps because of the well-known failure of the Hague Conventions of 1899 and 1907 to outlaw in practice the aerial bombardment of civilian targets, one of the chief causes of suffering in war during the twentieth century. On the other hand, the 1925 Geneva Protocol re-stating the Hague prohibition of the use of gas in war was observed throughout the Second World War, as it was not in the First, and has been ever since; the two serious breaches of the Protocol, by the Italians in Ethiopia in 1936 and by Saddam Hussein inside Iraq, attracted universal condemnation.

Last year another international agreement, signed by almost every state in the world, prohibited the use of anti-personnel mines and I expect it eventually to achieve the same force as that outlawing chemical agents. I would further predict the eventual abolition of other abhorrent weapons, such as blinding lasers, cluster missiles and high-fragmentation projectiles.

We must, however, be realistic about war's current reality and that entails admitting to pessimism as well as optimism. Particular causes for pessimism are supplied by the spectacle of warmaking between poor states which should find better ways to spend their money and by the rise of what is now called non-state warfare. Both are undeniable phenomena. While the old-established states, particularly those of Western Europe and North America, have been transforming themselves from belligerent to benevolent entities, many of the newer states, particularly those brought into being by the dissolution of European empires, have been unable to liberate themselves from the grip of internal hostilities that pre-date colonisation, or from external animosities against former colonial neighbours that the rule of empire held in check.

European ideologies, acquired through colonisation, are another cause of both external and internal enmities, as, for example, in Cambodia, where the requirement of adherence to an extreme form of Marxism led to the death of two million people; there the chilling preliminary to the murder of those judged politically incorrect took the form of an invitation to 'Come with us for further study'. In other societies, the disappointment of economic and political hopes aroused by liberation has resulted in the reinterpretation of religious belief in an aggressive and specifically anti-Western form. Terrorists inspired by Islamic fundamentalism have convinced themselves that the economic woes their societies suffer are caused by a Western conspiracy to keep them in poverty. Tragically, such convictions may resolve, as in Algeria, into bloody warfare between those factions which seek national revival through modernisation and those which appear to reject modernisation altogether.

But it is not just economic well-being that dampens the causes of conflict. The most intransigent conflicts of all have arisen in regions of very ancient mixed ethnicities, as in former Yugoslavia and in Caucasia. There the withdrawal of superordinate authority has cast the populations back into a condition which, though anthropologists disagree over whether what they call primitive warfare is primordial or not, is certainly a regression from civilised order. The practices of territorial displacement, massacre, deliberate desecration of cultural symbols and systematic mistreatment of women, all evidently rife in the recent non-state warfare in the Balkans and Transcaucasia, undeniably resemble those of the surviving Stone Age peoples of the world's remote regions, at their most savage.

It does appear then that economic poverty or instability, and cultural insecurity, each feed the belligerence of such states. But we need also to consider – alongside the characteristics of current warfare – the means by which it is waged. War is increasingly becoming an activity undertaken by poor rather than rich states; and neither non-state warfare nor warfare between poor states would trouble the world's conscience or threaten its stability were it not for the ready availability of cheap weapons. Since it is poor states which mainly cause war, the availability of cheap weapons is one of the most alarming ingredients of our contemporary military condition.

From the age of the chariot, three thousand years ago, to that of the dreadnought battleship, which came and went early in this century, military power belonged to those who could pay most. Today, the costliest weapons – nuclear weapons apart – are of little utility, except in the most particular circumstances. The supersonic jet fighter, for example, confers air superiority, but counts only in wars where air superiority is critical, and they are few. As a contributor to the toll of human death in warfare, the supersonic fighter scarcely figures; its role equates with that of the Formula One racing car in the computation of road traffic fatalities.

The mass-produced assault rifle, costing one-millionth of the jet fighter's price, is, by contrast, an almost universal scourge. Many of the fifty million dead of the wars of this century's second half have been killed by the cheap assault rifle. Its high rate of fire makes it deadly against the many in the hands of an individual, while its lightness and simplicity allow even untrained children – who figure increasingly frequently in the ranks of unofficial armies – to kill with a profligacy the veteran of the past could not achieve.

So abundant and so cheap are cheap weapons that I believe we ought now to consider, as a matter of urgency, whether the next initiative in the international disarmament endeavour should not be that of restricting their distribution and eventually their production. It is not true that the trade in cheap arms is a private commercial enterprise. Most cheap weapons have been released into the market by governments, often for political rather than commercial reasons. Some of the governments involved in the arms trade, it must be admitted, are those of impoverished ex-Soviet bloc states, seeking to raise cash by disposing of obsolete weapons or by sustaining the output of redundant industry. Others, working at the economic margin, have simply recognised that the demand for cheap weapons supplies a niche they can fill.

Either way – whether the trade in arms has a political or an economic motive – it is chiefly a government activity and, that being the case, and given that the trade's results are so wholly deplorable, the more secure, influential and responsible governments ought now to combine to bring it under control. If it has been possible to terminate the production of chemical weapons and, as seems now probable, that of anti-personnel mines, the restriction of the trade in cheap small-arms is attainable also.

We should not, however, delude ourselves that the progressive restriction of arms production and distribution will of itself rid the world of war. Disarmament is a necessary step in that direction, demonstrated by the low level of murder in states prohibiting the private possession of firearms. In those regions where significant measures of arms control, disarmament and reduction in the size of armed forces have been achieved, the infrequency, indeed total absence of armed conflict is also noticeable. Such regions are now extensive and extending. The military map of the globe, by comparison with that which might have been drawn at almost any earlier time in this century, shows little war and much peace. Those dedicated to the disarmament movement, at national, international and supranational level, may take credit for that.

We must recognise, however, that those who want weapons will usually acquire them – by improvisation or by traffic on the commercial or political black market – and that, as a result, those who want to fight will do so. That has been the case recently in areas of high ethnic hatred – many of the 800,000 Tutsi killed in Rwanda were hacked or bludgeoned to death – and in areas of political disintegration. The civil war in former Yugoslavia, a country that sustained an arms industry wholly disproportionate to its size, was carried on with weapons looted from national arsenals or fed into the conflict by interested external parties.

In such circumstances, and until the distribution of cheap weapons can be brought under stricter control, how should the enemies of war act? Act they must, for the waging of low-level war is no more in the interest of responsible governments than is the waging of high-level war. They should begin, I think, by recognising that culpability for the form war has so frequently taken in the recent past, and too often takes at present, belongs in part to them. The decision of the great powers, taken during the struggle against Hitler, to arm guerrilla and partisan forces and to raise civil war as a means of bringing him down set an example easily followed, as it has been by national liberation movements and now by fundamentalists and ethnic extremists around the globe. The encouragement of subversion as a strategy was short-sighted and the long-term price is now being paid. The price is paid through the evasion of the ideal of honour as the warrior virtue, an erosion that has once again made unfair fight, sabotage, assassination and massacre acceptable means of waging war.

War is a protean activity, by which I mean that it changes form, often unpredictably. It is for that reason that I have avoided attempting to define the nature of war throughout these lectures. Like disease, it exhibits the capacity to mutate, and mutates fastest in the face of efforts to control or eliminate it. War is collective killing for some collective purpose; that is as far as I would go in attempting to describe it. The Second War culminated with the deployment of a weapon, the ultimate weapon so-called, designed to rob collective killing of any logical purpose whatsoever. The nuclear weapon did indeed seem a final antidote and it has proved, thus far, a homoeopathic antidote against itself. It has not proved an antidote against the use of other weapons in the mutant forms war has taken since Hiroshima.

To what antidotes should we look? We should recall that war is now illegal, except in self-defence or unless sanctioned by the United Nations, and the elaboration of international law as it affects war is a profitable direction in which to move. The institution of a permanent court at the Hague empowered to try and punish war criminals has been a creative development. The progressive extension of the peace-keeping and peace-making activities of the United Nations Organisation itself is the most important of institutional antidotes. The UN has its critics and its failings, and events in Iraq this year have drawn fresh attention to its role. Yet without its machinery, and the powers given to it by international consent in its charter, the world would be far less well-equipped to avert, control and limit war than it is. Regional supranational organisations, specific non-aggressive in purpose or in effect, also have important roles to play, as do external mediators acting from goodwill and *ad hoc* peace-making or peace-keeping coalitions.

Since we know that poor states which have a fragile cultural identity are far more likely to engage in warmongering or to experience inter-ethnic conflict as a by-product of insecurity, what then can be done to secure their identity and economic well-being? Can we somehow help those fledgeling states to reach a more mature and stable condition of political security and economic autonomy? An essential weapon in our war against conflict must, therefore, be progress in aid and development programmes allied to stronger alliances with other nations which strengthen the economic structures of such states and help to neutralise the political insecurities against which their governments constantly battle. Only then can we help them also to reject, as we have done, Heraclitus's belief that strife is the only just and corrective force.

For in the last resort it will not be law nor the machinery for its administration that will keep the world's peace. And despite our best efforts, if war is to be driven to and beyond the horizon of civilisation, it will be because the United Nations retains both the will to confront unlawful force with lawful force and because the governments that lend it lawful force continue to train, pay and equip men of honour to carry out their orders. The call of honour is burdensome, often dangerous, always badly rewarded.

Those who discharge it, and I know them well, for I have spent most of my adult life in their company, are usually also misunderstood. Waging war when they must, warriors are suspected by the many to have an interest in war as an end in itself. Nothing could be further from the truth. No one doubts the utility of war more than the professional warrior, no one shuns it more actively. 'Violence rarely settles anything' are the most memorable words I have ever heard, because they were spoken to me by a former Chief of Defence Staff, our country's most senior serviceman. Equally, both he and I know that there are some things that, when the threat of violence has failed, can be settled by violence alone.

Violence is the most terrible instrument that the rule of law can take into its use. If we hope to see war driven towards its end, we must not shrink from seeing its causes addressed. Equally, we must not shrink from seeing violence used – nor from according honour to those honourable warriors who administer force in the cause of peace.

SELECT BIBLIOGRAPHY

Adam, P. *The Arts of the Third Reich*, London, 1992

Andreski, S. *Military Organisation and Society*, London, 1908

Anglesey, Marquess of *A History of British Cavalry*, IV, London, 1986

Ardrey, R. *The Territorial Imperative*, London, 1967

Ayalon, D. *Gunpowder and Firearms in the Mamluk Kingdom*, London, 1956

Azzarolli, A. *An Early History of Horsemanship*, London, 1985

Balsdon, J. *Rome*, London, 1970

Bar-Kochva, B. *The Seleucid Army*, Cambridge, 1976

Barnett, C. (ed.) *Hitler's Generals*, London, 1989

Bartov, O. *The Eastern Front 1941–5*, Basingstoke, 1985

Beaumont, J. *Comrades in Arms*, London, 1980

Beeler, J. *War in Feudal Europe*, 730–1200, Ithaca, 1991

Beloff, N. *Tito's Flawed Legacy*, London, 1985

Berlin, I. *Karl Marx*, Oxford, 1978

Berlin, I. *The Crooked Timber of Humanity*, NY, 1991

Best, G. *Humanity in Warfare*, London, 1980

Blau, P. and Scott, W. *Formal and Informal Organisations*, San Francisco, 1962

Blondal, S. *The Varangians of Byzantium*, Cambridge, 1979

Bottero, J. et al (eds.) *The Near East: the Early Civilisations*, London, 1967

Bramson, L. and Goethals, G. *War: Studies from Psychology, Sociology, Anthropology*, New York, 1964

Breeze, D. and Dobson, B. *Hadrian's Wall*, London, 1976

Breuil, H. and Lautier, R. *The Men of the Old Stone Age*, London, 1965

Bull, H. et al (eds.) *Hugo Grotius and International Relations*, Oxford, 1990

Bullock, A. *Hitler and Stalin*, London, 1991

Bury, J. *A History of the Later Roman Empire*, London, 1923

Callwell, C. *Small Wars, Their Principles and Practice*, London, 1899

Challener, R. *The French Theory of the Nation in Arms*, New York, 1955

Chevallier, R. *Roman Roads*, London, 1976

Clark, R. *Freud*, London, 1980

Clausewitz, Carl von, *On War* (tr. M. Howard and P. Paret), Princeton, 1976

Clausewitz, Carl von *On War* (tr. J. J. Graham), London, 1908

Clendinnen, I. *Ambivalent Conquests, Maya and Spaniard in Yucatan, 1515–70*, Cambridge 1987

Clendinnen, I. *Aztecs*, Cambridge, 1991

Connaughton, R. *The War of the Rising Sun and the Tumbling Bear*, London, 1988

Contamine, P. *War in the Middle Ages* (tr. M. Jones), Oxford, 1984

Corvisier, A. 'Le moral des combattants, panique et enthousiasme' in *Revue historique des armées*, 3, 1977

Corvisier, A. *Armies and Society in Europe*, Bloomington, Ill., 1979

Creel, H. *The Origins of Statecraft in China*, Chicago, 1970

Dawkin, J. *The Selfish Gene*, Oxford, 1989

de la Croix, H. *Military Considerations in City Planning*, New York, 1972

Deakin, F. *The Embattled Mountain*, London, 1971

Derry, T. and Williams, T. *A Short History of Technology*, Oxford, 1960

Divale, W. *War in Primitive Society*, Santa Barbara, 1973

Djilas, M. *Wartime*, New York, 1977

Doyle, W. *The Oxford History of the French Revolution*, Oxford, 1989

Duffy, C. *Russia's Military Way to the West*, London, 1981

Duffy, C. *Siege Warfare*, London, 1979

Duffy, C. *The Military Experience in the Age of Reason*, London, 1987

Dupuy, R. and T. *The Encyclopaedia of Military History*, London, 1986

Edburg, P. *Crusade and Settlement*, Cardiff, 1985

Edmonds, J. *A Short History of World War I*, Oxford, 1951

Eksteins, M. *Rites of Spring*, New York, 1989

Elting, J. *Swords Around a Throne*, London, 1989

Engels, D. *Alexander the Great and the Logistics of the Macedonian Army*, Berkeley, 1978

Englein, S. *Islands at The Centre of the World*, NY, 1990

Fames, O. *War in the Arctic*, London, 1991

Ferguson, B. and Whitehead, N. *War in the Tribal Zone*, Sante Fe, 1991

Ferguson, R. (ed.) *Warfare, Culture and Environment*, Orlando, 1984

Ferrill, A. *The Fall of the Roman Empire*, London, 1986

Ferrill, A. *The Origins of War*, London, 1985

Finley, M. and Plaket, H. *The Olympic Games*, New York, 1976

Forbes, P. J. *Metallurgy in Antiquity*, Leiden, 1950

Fox, A. *Prehistoric Maori Fortifications*, Auckland, 1974

Fraser, A. *Boadicea's Chariot*, London, 1988

Freedman, F. *The Evolution of Nuclear Strategy*, London, 1989

Freeman, D. *Margaret Mead and Samoa*, Cambridge, Mass., 1983

Fried, M. *Transactions of New York Academy of Sciences*, Series 2, 28, 1966

Fried, M., Harris, M. and Murphy, R. (eds.) *War: The Anthropology of Armed Conflict and Aggression*, New York, 1967

Friendly, A. *The Dreadful Day*, London, 1981

Fryer, J. *The Great Wall of China*, London, 1975

Fuller, J. *The Decisive Battles of the Western World*, London, 1954–6

Gabriel, R. and Metz, K. *From Sumer to Rome*, New York, 1991

Galvin, J. *The Minute Men*, McLean, Ill., 1989

Garlan, Y. *War in the Ancient World*, London, 1975

Gernet, J. *A History of Chinese Civilisation*, Cambridge, 1982

Gilbert, M. *Second World War*, London, 1989

Girouard, M. *The Return of Camelot*, New Haven, 1981

Grant, M. *The Army of the Caesars*, London, 1974

Greenhalgh, K. *Early Greek Warfare*, Cambridge, 1973

Groebel, J. and Hinde, R. (eds.) *Aggression and War*, Cambridge, 1989

Guilmartin, J. *Gunpowder and Galleys*, Cambridge, 1974

Haas, J. (ed.) *The Anthropology of War*, Cambridge, 1990

Hale, J. *Renaissance War Studies*, London, 1988

Hale, J. *War and Society in Renaissance Europe*, Leicester, 1985

Hammond, J. *A History of Greece to 322 B.C.*, Oxford, 1959

Hanson, V. (ed.) *Hoplites*, London, 1991

Hanson, V. *The Western Way of War*, New York, 1989

Hanson, V. *Warfare and Agriculture in Classical Greece*, Pisa, 1983

Harris, M. *The Rise of Anthropological Theory*, London, 1968

Harris, W. *War and Imperialism in Republican Rome*, Oxford, 1979

Hayes, W. 'Egypt from the Death of Ammanemes II to Seqemenre II' in *Cambridge Ancient History*, 3rd ed., Vol. II, Part 1

Hoffman, M. *Egypt Before the Pharaohs*, London, 1988

Hogg, A. *Hill Forts of Britain*, London, 1975

Holt, P., Lambion, A., and Lewis B. (eds.) *The Cambridge History of Islam*, Vol IA, Cambridge, 1970

Home, A. *A Savage War of Peace*, London, 1977

Horne, A. *To Lose a Battle*, London, 1969

Hourani, A. *A History of the Arab Peoples*, London, 1991

Howard, M. *Clausewitz*, Oxford, 1983

Howard, M. *War in European History*, Oxford, 1976

Hughes, Q. *Military Architecture*, London, 1974

Isaac, B. *The Limits of Empire*, Oxford, 1990

Jakobsen, J. and Adams, R. 'Salt and Silt in Ancient Mesopotamian Agriculture', *Science*, CXXVIII, 1958

Jefferson, G. *The Destruction of the Zulu Kingdom*, London, 1979

Jelavich, B. *History of the Balkans (Twentieth Century)*, Cambridge, 1983

Johnson, S. *Late Roman Fortifications*, London, 1983

Johnson, S. *Roman Fortifications on the Saxon Shore*, London, 1977

Jones, A. *The Decline of the Ancient World*, London, 1966

Jones, A. *The Later Roman Empire*, Oxford, 1962

Jones, C. *The Longman Companion to the French Revolution*, London, 1989

Jones, G. *A History of the Vikings*, Oxford, 1984

Jones, N. *Hitler's Heralds*, London, 1987

Kahn, D. *Seizing the Enigma*, London, 1991

Keegan, J. *The Mask of Command*, London, 1987

Keegan, J. *The Face of Battle*, London, 1976

Keegan, J. *The Price of Admiralty*, London, 1988

Keegan, J. *A History of Warfare*, London, 1993

Kemp, B. *Ancient Egypt, Anatomy of a Civilisation*, London, 1983

Kenny, A. *The Logic of Deterrence*, London, 1985

Keppie, L. *The Making of the Roman Army*, London, 1984

Kierman, F. and Fairbank, J. *Chinese Ways in Warfare*, Cambridge, Mass., 1974

Kirch, P. *The Evolution of the Polynesian Chiefdoms*, Cambridge, 1984

Klopsteg, P. *Turkish Archery and the Composite Bow*, Evanstown, 1947

Krige, E. J. *The Social System of the Zulus*, Pietermaritzburg, 1950

Kuper, A. *Anthropologists and Anthropology*, London, 1973

Kwantem, L. *Imperial Nomads: A History of Central Asia, 500–1500*, Leicester, 1979

Laessoe, J. *People of Ancient Assyria*, London, 1963

Larson, R. *The British Army and the Theory of Armoured Warfare 1918–40*, Newark, 1984

Lattimore, O. *Studies in Frontier History*, London, 1962

Lewis, M. *The Navy of Britain*, London, 1948

Liddell Hart, B. *The Ghost of Napoleon*, London, 1933

Liddle, P. *The 1916 Battle of the Somme*, London, 1992

Lindner, R. 'Nomadism, Horses and Huns', *Past and Present*, 1981

Livermore, T. *Numbers and Losses in the American Civil War*, Bloomington, Ill., 1957

Longmate, N. *Hitler's Rockets*, London, 1985

Lorenz, K. *On Aggression*, London, 1966

Lucas, J. *Fighting Troops of the Austro-Hungarian*

Army, New York, 1987

Luttwak, E. *The Grand Strategy of the Roman Empire*, Baltimore, 1976

Lynn, J. *Tools of War*, Chicago, 1990

Maenchen-Helfen, M. *The World of the Huns*, Berkeley, 1973

Mallet, M. *Mercenaries and Their Masters*, London, 1974

Mansel, P. *Pillers of Monarchy*, London, 1984

Manz, B. *The Rise and Rule of Tamerlane*, Cambridge, 1989

Marsol, A. *Egypt in the Reign of Muhammad Ali*, Cambridge, 1982

McCormick, L. and Perry, H. *Images of War*, London, 1991

McNeal, R. *Tsar and Cossack*, Basingstoke, 1989

McNeill, *The Pursuit of Power*, Oxford, 1983

McNeill, W. *A World History*, New York, 1961

McNeill, W. *Plagues and People*, New York, 1976

McNeill, W. *The Human Condition*, Princeton, 1980

McNeill, W. *The Rise of the West*, Chicago, 1963

McPherson, J. *Battle Cry of Freedom*, NY, 1988

Middleton, J. and Tait, D. *Tribes Without Rulers*, London, 1958

Milward, A. *War, Economy and Society, 1939–45*, London, 1977

Mockler, A. *Haile Selassie's War*, Oxford, 1979

Moorey, P. (ed.) *The Origins of Civilisation*, Oxford, 1979

Mueller, J. 'Changing Attitudes to War. The Impact of the First World War', *British Journal of Political Science*, 21

Murphy, T. (ed.) *The Holy War*, Columbus, 1976

Murray, W. *Luftwaffe*, London, 1985

Needham, J. *Science and Civilisation in China*, I, Cambridge, 1954

Nicolson, N. *Alex*, London, 1973

Oakeshott, E. *The Archaeology of Weapons*, London, 1960

Obermaier, H. *La vida de nuestros antepasados cuateranos en Europa*, Madrid, 1926

Oget, B. (ed.) *War and Society in Africa*, 1972

Pallud, J-P. *Blitzkrieg in the West*, London, 1991

Paret, P. (ed.) *Makers of Modern Strategy*, Princeton, 1986

Paret, P. *Clausewitz and the State*, Princeton, 1985

Paret, P. *Understanding War*, Princeton, 1992

Parker, G. *The Army of Flanders and the Spanish Road*, Cambridge, 1972

Parker, G. *The Military Revolution*, Cambridge, 1988

Parker, G. and A. *European Soldiers 1550–1650*, Cambridge, 1977

Parkinson, R. *Clausewitz*, London, 1970

Parry, V. and Yapp, M. (eds.) *War, Technology and Society in the Middle East*, London, 1975

Perrin, N. *Giving Up the Gun*, Boston, 1988

Petite, D. *Le balcon de la Côte d'Azure*, Marignan, 1983

Piekalkiewicz, J. *Pferd und Reiter im II Weltkrieg*, Munich, 1976

Piggott, S. *The Earliest Wheeled Transport*, London, 1983

Pipes, D. *Slave Soldiers and Islam*, New Haven, 1981

Poliakoff, M. *Combat Sports in the Ancient World*, New Haven, 1987

Pounds, N. *The Mediaeval Castle in England and Wales*, Cambridge, 1990

Ratchnevsky, P. *Genghis Khan*, Oxford, 1991

Reid, W. *Arms Through the Ages*, New York, 1976

Robarchak, C. in *Papers Presented to the Guggenheim Foundation Conference, On the Anthropology of War*, Santa Fe, 1986

Roberts, J. *The Pelican History of the World*, London, 1987

Roeder, H. (ed.) *The Ordeal of Captain Roeder*, London, 1960

Roux, G. *Ancient Iraq*, New York, 1986

Royle, T. *A Dictionary of Military Quotations*, London, 1990

Runciman, S. *A History of the Crusades*, I, Cambridge, 1951

Saggs, H. *The Might That Was Assyria*, London, 1984

Sahlins, M. *Tribesmen*, NJ, 1968

Sainty, G. *The Order of St John*, New York, 1991

Sallares, R. *The Ecology of the Ancient Greek World*, London, 1991

Sanders, N. *The Sea Peoples*, London, 1985

Sansom, G. *The Western World and Japan*, London, 1950

Sansome, D. *Greek Athletics and the Genesis of Sport*, Berkeley, 1988

Saunders, J. *The History of the Mongol Conquest*, London, 1971

Saxe, Marshal de *Mes rêveries*, Amsterdam, 1757

Seaton, A. *The Horsemen of the Steppes*, London, 1985

Showalter, D. *Railroads and Rifles*, Hamden, 1975

Smail, R. *Crusading Warfare*, Cambridge, 1956

Spector, R. *Eagle Against the Sun*, London, 1984

Spence, J. *The Search for Modern China*, London, 1990

Spuler, B. *The Mongols in History*, London, 1971

St. Clair, W. *That Greece Might Still Be Free*, London, 1972

Stahlberg, A. *Bounden Duty*, London, 1990

Storrey, R. *A History of Modern Japan*, London, 1960

Taylor, T. *The Breaking Wave*, London, 1967

Terraine, J. *The Right of the Line*, London, 1985

Thomas, H. *An Unfinished History of the World*, London, 1979

Thompson, J. *No Picnic*, London, 1992

Thompson, J. *The Lifeblood of War*, London, 1991

Tiger, L. and Fox, R. *The Imperial Animal*, London, 1972

Tolstoy, L. *Anna Karenin* (tr. R. Edmonds), London, 1987

Turney-High, H. *Primitive War: Its Practice and Concepts* (2nd edn), Columbia, SC 1971

Van Crefeld, M. *Technology and War*, London, 1991

Van der Heyden, A. and Scullard, H. (eds.) *Atlas of the Classical World*, London, 1959

Van der Vat, D. *The Atlantic Campaign*, London, 1988

Vayda, A. *War in Ecological Perspective*, New York, 1976

Wakefield, K. (ed.) *The Blitz Then and Now*, London, 1988

Waldron, A. *The Great Wall of China*, Cambridge, 1992

Watson, G. *The Roman Soldier*, London, 1985

Weigley, R. *The Age of Battles*, Bloomington, Ill., 1991

Welchman, G. *The Hut Six Story*, London, 1982

Wendorf, F. (ed.) *The Prehistory of Nubia*, II, Dallas, 1968

Wiley, B. *The Life of Johnny Reb*, Baton Rouge, 1918

Wilson, T. *The Myriad Faces of War*, Cambridge, 1986

Winter, F. *Greek Fortifications*, Toronto, 1971

Wintle, J. *The Dictionary of War Quotations*, London, 1989

Wood, E. *Peasant, Citizen and Slave*, London, 1988

Ya-tien, Chen *Chinese Military Theory*, Stevenage, 1992

Yadin, Y. *The Art of Warfare in Biblical Lands*, London, 1963

"John Keegan is at once the most readable and the most original of living historians."   —*The New York Times Book Review*

FIELDS OF BATTLE

Spanning more than two centuries and the expanse of a continent, Keegan shows how the immense spaces of North America shaped the battles and wars that were fought on its soil. He revisits fields of combat from Quebec to Little Bighorn and retraces Washington's triumph and McClellan's defeat at Virginia battlefields only a few miles apart. Once again, Keegan's scholarship gives Americans a brilliant reassessment of their military heritage.

History/0-679-74664-1

THE FIRST WORLD WAR

In this magisterial narrative, Keegan has produced the definitive account of the Great War. He sheds fascinating light on weaponry and technology, shows us the doomed negotiations between the monarchs and ministers of 1914, and takes us into the verminous trenches of the Western front. His brilliant, panoramic account of this vast and terrible conflict is destined to take its place among the classics of world history.

History/0-375-70045-5

THE BATTLE FOR HISTORY

Re-fighting World War II

In this engaging and concise volume, Keegan evaluates books that range from general histories to biographies of the war's principal figures, from accounts of individual campaigns to studies of espionage and resistance. What emerges is a book that combines stunning erudition with crisp prose—a thought provoking work for any serious student of World War II.

History/0-679-76743-6

Analyzing centuries of conflict—in societies from those of the Amazon to the Balkans—Keegan unveils the deepest motives behind humanity's penchant for mass bloodshed. *A History of Warfare* is a masterpiece of military scholarship, irresistible in its style and terrifying in its implications.

History/0-679-73082-6

VINTAGE BOOKS
Available at your local bookstore, or call toll-free to order:
1-800-793-2665 (credit cards only)